CHILDHOOD

The sociology of childhood has a relatively short history, yet it has grown as an area of academic and policy interest in recent years. The social sciences previously handled childhood either through theories of socialization or through developmental psychology – both of which have led to children being considered as a natural rather than social phenomenon.

Childhood offers a greater appreciation of the social factors that make up our knowledge of children and childhood. It gives a critical framework through which to understand private attitudes and public policy in relation to the child, viewing childhood from a social constructionist perspective.

The basic assumption that childhood is a social construct reveals that our understandings of childhood and the meanings that we place upon children vary considerably from culture to culture, but also quite radically within the history of any one culture.

Chris Jenks is both Reader in Sociology and Head of the Department of Sociology at Goldsmiths' College, University of London.

KEY IDEAS
Series Editor: Peter Hamilton
The Open University

KEY IDEAS
Series Editor: PETER HAMILTON
The Open University, Milton Keynes

Designed to complement the successful *Key Sociologists*, this series
covers the main concepts, issues, debates, and controversies in
sociology and the social sciences. The series aims to provide
authoritative essays on central topics of social science, such as
community, power, work, sexuality, inequality, benefits and ideology,
class, family, etc. Books adopt a strong individual 'line' constituting
original essays rather than literary surveys, and form lively and original
treatments of their subject matter. The books will be useful to students
and teachers of sociology, political science, economics, psychology,
philosophy, and geography.

THE SYMBOLIC CONSTRUCTION OF COMMUNITY
ANTHONY P. COHEN, Department of Social Anthropology,
University of Manchester
SOCIETY
DAVID FRISBY and DEREK SAYER, Department of Sociology,
University of Manchester
SEXUALITY
JEFFREY WEEKS, Social Work Studies Department, University of
Southampton
WORKING
GRAEME SALAMAN, Faculty of Social Sciences, The Open
University, Milton Keynes
BELIEFS AND IDEOLOGY
KENNETH THOMPSON, Faculty of Social Sciences, The Open
University, Milton Keynes
EQUALITY
BRYAN TURNER, School of Social Sciences, The Flinders University
of South Australia
HEGEMONY
ROBERT BOCOCK, Faculty of Social Sciences, The Open University,
Milton Keynes
RACISM
ROBERT MILES, Department of Sociology, University of Glasgow
POSTMODERNITY
BARRY SMART, Associate Professor of Sociology, University of
Auckland, New Zealand
CULTURE
CHRIS JENKS, Department of Sociology, Goldsmiths' College,
University of London

CHILDHOOD

CHRIS JENKS

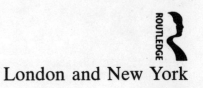

London and New York

First published 1996
by Routledge
11 New Fetter Lane, London EC4P 4EE

Simultaneously published in the USA and Canada
by Routledge
29 West 35th Street, New York, NY 10001

Reprinted 1997

© 1996 Chris Jenks

Phototypeset in Times by Intype London Ltd
Printed and bound in Great Britain by Clays Ltd, St. Ives PLC

British Library Cataloguing in Publication Data
A catalogue for this book is available from the British Library

Library of Congress Cataloguing in Publication Data
Jenks, Chris.
    Childhood / Chris Jenks.
       p.   cm. — (Key ideas)
    Includes bibliographical references and index.
    1. Children.   2. Children—Social conditions.   I. Title.
    II. Series.
    HQ767.9.J45   1996
    305.23—dc20   95-33686
                                                                  CIP

ISBN 0–415–12013–6 (hbk)
ISBN 0–415–12014–4 (pbk)

For my mum and dad,
with love and gratitude

Contents

1
Constituting childhood

We would not have our Guardians grow up among representations of
moral deformity, as in some foul pasture where, day after day, feeding
on every poisonous weed they would, little by little, gather insensibly a
mass of corruption in their very souls. Rather we must seek out those
craftsmen whose instinct guides them to whatsoever is lovely and
gracious; so that our young men, dwelling in a wholesome climate,
may drink in good from every quarter, whence, like a breeze bearing
health from happy regions, some influence from noble works constantly
falls upon eye and ear from childhood upward, and imperceptibly draws
them into sympathy and harmony with the beauty of reason, whose
impress they take. Hence . . . the decisive importance of education in
poetry and music; rhythm and harmony sink deep into the recesses of
the soul and take the strongest hold there, bringing that grace of body
and mind which is only to be found in one who is brought up in the right
way. Moreover, a proper training in this kind makes a man quick to
perceive any defects or ugliness in art or in nature. Such deformity
will rightly disgust him. Approving all that is lovely, he will welcome it
home with joy into his soul and, nourished thereby, grow into a man
of noble spirit. All that is ugly and disgraceful he will rightly condemn
and abhor while he is still too young to understand the reason; and when
reason comes, he will greet her as a friend with whom his education has
made him long familiar.

Plato, *The Republic*

In what ways can we possibly begin to make sense of children? This is by no means a novel question. Since humankind first achieved parenthood the problem has stalked the adult condition. But at a different level we might rightly suppose that from the earliest Socratic dialogue onwards through the history of ideas, moral, social and political theorists have systematically endeavoured to constitute a view of the child that is compatible with their particular visions of social life and continuous with their speculations concerning the future. Beginning from that initial Hellenic desire to seek out the origins of virtue in order to instil rhythm and harmony into the very souls of the young, and extending up until our contemporary pragmatic concerns with the efficacy of specific and fashionable child-rearing practices, after centuries of debate and practice, we have still not achieved any consensus over the issue of childhood. Despite a long cultural commitment to the good of the child and a more recent intellectual engagement with the topic of childhood, what remains perpetually diffuse and ambiguous is the basic conceptualization of childhood as a social practice. Childhood remains largely unrealized as an emergent patterning of action. As Rousseau stated in the Preface to *Émile*:

> We know nothing of childhood: and with our mistaken notions the further we advance the further we go astray. The wisest writers devote themselves to what a man ought to know, without asking what a child is capable of learning. They are always looking for the man in the child, without considering what he is before he becomes a man.

What do we bring to mind when we contemplate the child? Whether to regard children as pure, bestial, innocent, corrupt, charged with potential, *tabula rasa*, or even as we view our adult selves; whether they think and reason as we do, are immersed in a receding tide of inadequacy, or are possessors of a clarity of vision which we have through experience lost; whether their forms of language, games and conventions are alternatives to our own, imitations or crude precursors of our own now outgrown, or simply transitory impenetrable trivia which are amusing to witness and recollect; whether they are constrained and we have achieved freedom, or we have assumed constraint and they are truly free – all these considerations, and more, continue to exercise our theorizing about the child in social life.

Any review of the multiplicity of perspectives that are emerging in relation to childhood and also those that have previously been adopted in this area of study reveal, at one level, a continuous paradox, albeit expressed in a variety of forms. Simply stated the child is familiar to us and yet strange, he or she inhabits our world and yet seems to answer to another, he or she is essentially of ourselves and yet appears to display a systematically different order of being. The child's serious purpose and our intentions towards him or her are dedicated to a resolution of that initial paradox by transforming him or her into an adult, like ourselves. The reflexive recognition of this sustained, and sustaining, commitment opens up the whole related set of questions concerning the necessity and contingency of the relationship between the child and the adult, both in theory and in everyday life. The 'known' difference between these two social locations directs us towards an understanding of the identity contained within each; the contents are marked by the boundaries. The child, therefore, cannot be imagined except in relation to a conception of the adult, but essentially it becomes impossible to generate a well-defined sense of the adult, and indeed adult society, without first positing the child. The relationship child–adult appears locked within the binary reasoning which, for so long, both contained and constrained critical thought in relation to issues of gender and ethnicity. The child, it would seem, has not escaped or deconstructed into the post-structuralist space of multiple and self-presentational identity sets.

From this formulation we may distil two elements that appear common to the mainstream of approaches to the study of childhood. First, a foundational belief that the child instances difference and particularity (a belief that we shall later explore), and second, following from the former, a universal cultural desire to both achieve and account for the integration of that difference into a more broadly conceived sense of order and generality that comprises adult society. This is an integration predicted and condemned by Rousseau:

> Nature wants children to be children before they are men. If we deliberately pervert this order, we shall get premature fruits which are neither ripe nor well-flavoured, and which soon decay.... Childhood has ways of seeing, thinking, and feeling peculiar to itself; nothing can be more foolish than to substitute our ways for them.

Typically, however, the overwhelming irony of this manner of thinking is that it signally fails to attend to, or even acknowledge, its own paradoxical character. Inevitably the child side of the relationship within analysis of this genre is uniformly recovered in a negative fashion. Such theories, which tend to be hegemonic within their specific disciplines, such as socialization theory and developmental psychology, are predicated upon a strong but unexplicated knowledge of the difference of childhood and they proceed rapidly to an overattentive elaboration of the compulsive processes of integration. It is as if the basic ontological questions, 'What is a child?' and 'How is the child possible as such?', were, so to speak, satisfactorily answered in advance of the theorizing and then summarily dismissed.

THE CHILD AS 'SAVAGE'

In many ways this constitutes a reprise of nineteenth-century social thought. Just as the early 'evolutionist' anthropologist, a self-styled civilized person, simply 'knew' the savage to be different to himself, on a scale of advancement, and thus worthy of study; so we also, as rational adults, recognize the child as different, less developed, and in need of explanation. Both of these positions proceed from a pre-established but tacit ontological theory, a theory of what makes up the being of the other, be it savage or child. It is these unspoken forms of knowledge, these tacit commitments to difference that routinely give rise to the accepted definition of the savage or the child as a 'natural' meaningful order of object. Such implicit theories serve to render the child–adult continuum as utterly conventional and thus taken for granted for the modern social theorist as the distinction between primitive thought and rational thought was for the early anthropologist. Such social hierarchies are taken for granted in our cognitions because we do not examine the assumptions on which they are based. These assumptions embody the values and interests of the theorist and the contemporary culture, which in turn generate normative expectations within the wider society. However, the history of the social sciences has attested to a sequential critical address and debunking of the dominant ideologies of capitalism in relation to social class, colonialism in relation to race, and patriarchy in relation to gender; but as yet the ideology of development in relation to childhood has remained relatively intact. The politics of this situation warrant further exploration; its consequences are that the child, like the savage of an earlier epoch, is either excluded from our analysis or reimported as an afterthought. A major concern of this book is to encourage the reader to make a critical reconstruction of such sets of assumptions as they may be available, and to different degrees, in the literature concerning childhood that we shall explore together. In this way the child might by reinvented or at least recovered positively. Cunningham contributes to this question when he states that: 'Analogies between children and savages do not exist in a social or political vacuum.' He seeks to relate such analogies precisely to their contexts or, to use his own terms 'to identify discourses about childhood, and the power relationships which they embody.'[1]

At risk of exhausting the previously developed analogy it may be suggested that whereas the early anthropologist had to voyage to his chosen phenomena, like an explorer, across social space, the child as a contemporary topic has been most vividly brought into recognition through the passage of social time. Both of these journeys symbolize a questing after control through understanding but neither are appropriately exclusive in as much as both the synchronic and diachronic dimensions are pertinent to our knowledge of any socio-cultural form. What we should recognize however, is that both such processes are significant in fashioning their object; that is to say, comparative and historical analyses, in different ways, succeeded in establishing different classifications and boundaries around their phenomena. The manner of our assembling and the character of our distancing are significant in the constitution of either savage or child. A range of histories of childhood that we shall examine later demonstrate the erratic evolution of the image of childhood and its changing modes of recognition and reception. We will note that the child emerges in contemporary European culture as a formal category and as a social status embedded in programmes of care, routines of surveillance and schemes of education and assessment. Such accounts ensure that the child is realized as the social construction of a particular historical context and this provides a major platform for much contemporary theorizing about childhood; however it is the child's identity as a social status that determines its difference and recognition in the everyday world. The status of childhood has its boundaries maintained through the crystallization of conventions and discourses into lasting institutional forms like families, nurseries, schools and clinics, all agencies specifically designed and established to process the child as a uniform entity. Comparative material drawn from cross-cultural contexts reveals divergent sets of conventions and discourses, and thus institutional forms, some utterly different from our own but others bearing strong resemblances, all are bound together through homology. The comparative material, as we shall see, instructs us to think more profitably of childhood(s) rather than of a singular and mono-dimensional status.

In the same way that the 'savage' served as the anthropologist's referent for humankind's elementary forms of organization and primitive classifications, thus providing a speculative sense of the primal condition of human being within the socio-cultural process, so also the child is taken to display for adults their own state of once untutored difference, but in a more collapsed form: a spectrum reduced from 'human history' to one of generations. It will be suggested that within the child humanity sees its immediate past but also contemplates the immortality of its immanent future.

In the everyday world the category of childhood is a totalizing concept, it concretely describes a community that at some time has everybody as its member. This is a community which is therefore relatively stable and wholly predictable in its structure but by definition only fleeting in its particular membership. Beyond this the category signifies a primary experience in the existential biography of each individual and thus inescapably derives its common-sense meanings, relevance and relation not only from what it might currently be as a social status but also from how each and every individual, at some time, must have been. It is the only truly common experience of being human, infant mortality is no disqualification.

THE 'NATURAL' CHILD

Perhaps because of this seemingly all-encompassing character of the phenomenon as a social status and because of the essentially personal character of its particular articulation, common-sense thinking and everyday language in contemporary society are rife with notions concerning childhood. Being a child, having been a child, having children and having continuously to relate to children are all experiences which contrive to render the category as 'normal' and readily transform our attribution of it to the realm of the 'natural' (as used to be the case with sex and race). Such understandings, within the collective awareness, are organized around the single most compelling metaphor of contemporary culture, that of 'growth'. Stemming from this, the physical signs of anatomical change that accompany childhood are taken to be indicators of a social transition, so that the conflation of the realms of the 'natural' and the 'social' is perpetually reinforced.

All contemporary approaches to the study of childhood are clearly committed to the view that childhood is not a natural phenomenon and cannot properly be understood as such. The social transformation from child to adult does not follow directly from physical growth and the recognition of children by adults, and vice versa, is not singularly contingent upon physical difference. Furthermore, physical morphology may constitute a form of difference between people in certain circumstances but it is not an adequately intelligible basis for the relationship between the adult and the child. Childhood is to be understood as a social construct, it makes reference to a social status delineated by boundaries that vary through time and from society to society but which are incorporated within the social structure and thus manifested through and formative of certain typical forms of conduct. Childhood then always relates to a particular cultural setting.

Our early anthropologist would readily recognize the significance of such concepts within the social life of his 'savage'; he would demonstrate that the variety and hierarchy of social statuses within the tribe are plainly prescribed by boundaries which are, in turn, maintained through conventional practices deeply bound within ritual. Any transposition from one status location to another is never simply a matter of physical growth or indeed physical change. Such movements require transformatory process such as valediction, rites of passage and initiation ceremonies, all of which are disruptive and painful and have an impact not just upon the individual but also upon the collectivity. The recognition that we are addressing the somewhat more diffuse and volatile boundaries that mark off childhood today, and the fact that we are considering such a transition from within the mores and folkways of a modern secular society, is no guarantee that the ritualism will be any less present. Rather, perhaps, the rituals will have become more deep-seated and ideological in their justification. Whatever, the experience of change through ritual will continue to exercise a violent and turbulent constraint on the individual's consciousness. We might argue, in fact, that since the turn of the twentieth century we have developed a psychoanalytic vocabulary of motives that ascribe all pathological conduct to the dysfunctional integration of the effects of the culturally based rituals that are instrumental in our becoming adult.

The widespread tendency to routinize and 'naturalize' childhood, both in common sense and in theory, serves to conceal its analytic importance behind a cloak of the mundane; its significance and 'strangeness' as a social phenomenon is obscured. Within everyday rhetoric and many discourses of theory childhood is taken for granted, it is regarded as necessary and inevitable, and thus part of normal life – its utter 'thereness' seems to foster a complacent attitude. This naturalism has, up until fairly recently, extended to the social sciences, particularly psychology, where childhood is apprehended largely in terms of biological and cognitive development through concepts such as 'maturation'. Sociology, in search of explanations through structural causality, has independently sought to understand the problem of the child's acquisition of specific cultural repertoires through the largely one-sided theories of socialization. All of these ways of proceeding, though predominant within the academy, leave the actual child untheorized, they all contrive to gloss over the social experience that is childhood. We might here concur with Hillman who, albeit writing in the context of pastoral psychology, states that much of what is said about children and childhood is not really about children and childhood at all.

> What is this 'child' – that is surely the first question. Whatever we say about children and childhood is not altogether about children and childhood. What is this peculiar realm we call 'childhood' and what are we doing by establishing a special world with children's rooms and children's toys, children's clothes, and children's books. Clearly, some realm of the psyche called 'childhood' is being personified by the child and carried by the child for the adult.[2]

THE 'SOCIAL' CHILD

I will suggest throughout this book that, in significant ways, the child, as conceptualized both within the spectrum of everyday attitudes and the professional discourses of the social sciences, is employed, consciously though often unconsciously, as a device to propound versions of sociality and social cohesion.

Understood from within a variety of disciplines and perspectives, and also across a range of different sets of interests, childhood receives treatment as a stage, a structured process of becoming, but rarely as a course of action or a coherent social practice. The type of 'growth' metaphors that are readily adopted in discussions about childhood all pertain to the character of what is yet to be and yet which is also presupposed. Thus childhood is spoken about as: a 'becoming'; as a *tabula rasa*; as laying down the foundations; as shaping the individual; taking on; growing up; preparation; inadequacy; inexperience; immaturity, and so on. Such metaphoricity all speaks of an essential and magnetic relation to an unexplicated, but nevertheless firmly established, rational adult world. This adult world is not only assumed to be complete, recognizable and in stasis, but also, and perhaps most significantly, desirable. It is a benevolent and coherent totality which extends a welcome to the child, it invites him to cast off the qualities that ensure his differences, and it encourages his acquiescence to the preponderance of the induction procedures that will guarantee his corporate identity.

For the anthropologist to proceed from such a stance would be for him to invite the charge of ethnocentrism, and deservedly so! If he were to suggest that the 'savage' was in some way in his shadow, acting through delusion, stupidity, intellectual inadequacy, or operating with a proto-typical form of his own 'advanced', 'developed' or 'civilized' cultural devices then he would be working against a backdrop of his own social standards, treated as necessarily pre-eminent and essentially morally superior. This intransigent encoding of his own cultural experience would thus become the central unexplored problem in the anthropologist's work, and his view of another person as a 'savage' would make direct reference to that analytic problem. In the same way any view of the child reflects a preferred, but unexplored, model of the social order. This is an issue it would be 'childish' to ignore ...

In keeping with this form of ethnocentrism (I am loath to coin the neologism 'gerontocentrism'), socialization theories present the normative structure of the adult/parent world as their independent variable. Even though all sociologists are aware that such a notion of normative structure is itself a highly problematic belief from which to begin, it is nevertheless treated as a yardstick in relation to the child. Against this yardstick of an assumed consensus of reality the child is judged to be more or less competent and consequently the continuous lived social practice of being a child with a specific and coherent meaning structure is wholly ignored. This unilateral manipulation of children within socialization theories condemns them to the permanent conceptual status of absent presence. Ironically in relation to their actual intrusions into the best-laid plans of adult aspiration, children are depotentiated within socialization theory, they become nominal ciphers seemingly without an active dimension. As Speier has stated:

> Sociology considers the social life of the child as a basic area of study in so-called institutional analyses of family and school, for example. What is classically problematic about studying children is the fact of cultural induction, as I might refer to it. That is, sociologists (and this probably goes for anthropologists and psychologists) commonly treat childhood as a stage of life that builds preparatory mechanisms into the child's behavior so that he is gradually equipped with the competence to participate in the everyday activities of his cultural partners, and eventually as a bona fide adult member himself. This classical sociological problem has been subsumed under the major heading of socialization.[3]

The ironies abound. Back to my original formulation, we note that although lay members systematically manage to establish childhood as a social category in its own right, most social theories, through their emphasis on a taken-for-granted adult world, spectacularly fail to constitute the child as an ontology in its own right. The grounds of the difference between children and adults are undisclosed; such theorizing is forgetful of its origins. The social practice emergent as childhood is, within socialization theories, without moment; it finds voice only as a distant echo of what it is yet to become.

All accounts of this character begin from an essential and given model of human conduct and then seek to explain childhood as if teleologically related to that pre-established end. In such a way socialization theories are dedicatedly unreflexive, they methodically fail to recognize or acknowledge their own intentional nature, which is ultimately the justification of particular social worlds. The interests and purposes inherent within such worlds remain undisclosed. This crucial point was well expressed by O'Neill when he stated that 'any theory of child socialization is implicitly a theory of a social reality if not a particular historical social order.'[4]

We can now, perhaps, begin to see that a persistent and deeper analytic theme, stemming from the emblematic role of childhood as an idea, is a more fundamental orientation towards the preservation of both social and sociological worlds. When we talk of the child we are also talking about recollections of time past, images of current forms of relationship and aspirations towards future states of affairs. All of these visions are accessible through the child and are mediated through a variety of forms as divergent as: tabloid accounts of Satanic abuse; the battles over the National Curriculum; the investment in and appeal of Disneyland; and the public reaction to the murder of Jamie Bulger, to name but a few. It is precisely because of this conceptual complex that any analysis of childhood must rigorously attempt to open up the boundaries that have been placed around the experience, whether such boundaries are commonsensical, sociological, educational, psychological, medical or biological in type. In this way it becomes increasingly possible to actually topicalize 'the child' for social theory.

It appears then that the constitution of the child presents a major problem for sociological formulations of collective life. Whenever a social world is assembled in theorizing it is traditionally populated by and articulated through 'normal', 'natural' and 'rational' models of human conduct – this convention stems from Hobbes and even before. Within sociological worlds, the implicit view of humankind, however specific and insular it may be, is consistently based on the assumption of a kind of behavioural totality, a sense of completeness and arrival. The rational acting member of such worlds personifies adulthood. All action within sociological worlds, if it is to be intelligible as such, gravitates inevitably towards a universal yet covert specification of rule, the rule of the social system. Even pathological behaviour, in whatever form, is integrated and managed, within the context of the theory, in terms of it being either a negatively oriented or an unreasonably stigmatized expression of adult behaviour. What we can note here, however, is that the child, childhood, child behaviour and child's play cannot be viewed adequately through the same overall explanatory devices. Sociological worlds are constructed in direct relation to beliefs about universal 'rational adults', yet our everyday experience as practical members of real social worlds abounds with children and the impact of the difference and divergence that they represent.

It could be suggested that, in a strong sense, the very possibilities of difference and divergence contained within childhood, understood either as a course of action or as a community, present a potentially disintegrative threat to sociological worlds. The issue is political. Childhood constitutes a way of conduct that cannot properly be evaluated and routinely incorporated within the grammar of existing social systems. It emerges almost as a struggle between old orders and new orders. It is in this regard that theory manoeuvres to envelop the child within its own parameters. Childhood is understood after the fact of successful social systems, it is treated as a residual category and incorporated through remedial theories of socialization.

The point is worthy of reiteration: childhood receives treatment through its archetypal image, it is conceptualized as a structured becoming, not a social practice nor as a location for the Self (however elusive post-structuralism may have rendered this concept). The archetype of the child is sustained in language and in the discourses of the professions, the institutions and the specialisms which serve to patrol the boundaries marked out around childhood as a social status. These boundaries do not simply delineate the extent and compass of the child in society but they do proscribe a social space which in turn, and at a different level, expresses the control component exercised in the framework of that social system and the control variant which reveals the interests that sustain its functioning. Thus in relation to the discourse of education Bernstein stated:

> How a society selects, classifies, distributes, transmits and evaluates the educational knowledge it considers to be public, reflects both the distribution of power and the principles of social control. From this point of view, differences within and changes in the organization, transmission and evaluation of educational knowledge should be a major area of sociological interest.[5]

The image of the child then, in and through language, presupposes and stands in relation to the 'interested' character of a structured adult world. The metaphoricity directs us towards an understanding of the moral basis of such interests – see, for example, the child as 'human capital'.

Literary and ethnographic accounts have explored the practical content of the child's difference, as for example Coveney: 'Until the last decade of the eighteenth century the child did not exist as an important and continuous theme in English literature. Childhood as a major theme came with the generation of Blake and Wordsworth.'[6] Also see Opie and Opie's exhaustive denotations of playground games, argot and folklore: 'The scraps of lore which children learn from each other are at once more real, more immediately serviceable, and vastly more entertaining to them than anything which they learn from grown-ups.'[7]

Such attempts to justify children as embodied, constructive and as considered in the occupation of a world of their own making are important empirical contributions. This kind of descriptive specification of a child's difference is, however, only a beginning. We need to look at the reasons for the child and the generative grounds of the image and the archetypes in our language.

SOCIALIZATION THEORY – THE PARSONIAN PARADIGM

The order of socialization theories so far discussed[8] begins from a specific and given model of the dominant social and cultural formation (which enshrines the theorist's purpose) and relentlessly strives to subvert and restructure the child's potentially dangerous and disruptive difference into a form that equates with the unexplicated grounds of the initial theorizing. The child's volatility is stabilized, its riotousness quelled. Such theoretic transformation generates what Wrong has termed 'the oversocialized conception of man':

> 'Socialization' may mean two quite distinct things; when they are confused an oversocialized view of man is the result. On the one hand socialization means the 'transmission of culture', the particular culture of the society an individual enters at birth; on the other hand the term is used to mean the 'process of becoming human' of acquiring uniquely human attributes from interaction with others. All men are socialized in the latter sense, but this does not mean that they have been completely moulded by the particular norms and values of their culture.'[9]

Such theoretic transformation can be experienced in its finest and most original form in the corpus of Talcott Parsons' *The Social System*:

> The term socialization in its current usage in the literature refers primarily to the process of child development. . . . However, there is another reason for singling out the socialization of the child. There is reason to believe that, among the learned elements of personality in certain respects the stablest and most enduring are the major value-orientation patterns and there is much evidence that these are 'laid down' in childhood and are not on a large scale subject to drastic alteration during adult life.[10]

Parsons' work establishes a magnificent structure of social organization integrating the dimensions of action and constraint – a monumental task indeed! This edifice operates at the levels of the economic, the political, the cultural, the interactional and the personal – it is thus intended to both permeate and saturate all expressions of collective human experience. Parsons' social system constitutes the oneness of the social world through two guiding metaphors: first that of 'organicism' which speaks of the unspecific, the living and is concerned with content; second that of a 'system' which makes reference to the explicit, the inanimate and is concerned with form. Through our central concept of socialization Parsons commits a theoretic violence, particularly upon the child, through seeking to convert their worlds from content to form. It is as if societies are conceived of as living organisms but are everywhere becoming machines. A prophetic and dystopian vision. To reinvoke my original terms, the social system seeks to transform or merge difference into communality.

Parsons' concerns are grounded in the Hobbesian problem of order, however, within the sociological tradition Hobbes' *Leviathan*, the monstrous form of the political state which provides for and simultaneously symbolizes the unity of the people, is supplanted by the concept of 'society'. Society becomes the monitor for all order and it further inculcates a set of rules of conduct which are enforced less by individual will and political sovereignty than by society's own pre-existence. This supra-individual monolith remains the unquestioned origin of all causality and all explanation within an order-based sociological tradition. O'Neill has formulated the problem thus:

We will uncover the archaeology of docility that runs from Plato's *Republic* through to Parsons' *Social System*. Such an inquiry does not discover a single strategy for the production of the docile citizen. Rather, what appears is a plurality of discursive strategies. . . . The two registers of docility reflect two sides of the same problem of social control, namely, how it is that individuals can be induced to commit themselves *morally* to a social order that seeks to bind them to itself *physically*, i.e., in virtue of its discovery of certain laws of association. The conventional wisdom holds that Parsons' structural functionalism sublimates the moral question in favour of its analytic resolution, overriding critical consciousness with the normative claims of social consensus. Whether from a Hobbesian or Freudian perspective, sociology has always flirted with the discovery of a social physics. . . . The dream of the social sciences lies in the search for control strategies that would overlap the micro and macro orders of behaviour in a single order of administration. . . . In other words, despite the analytic power of the Parsonian vision, the discipline of sociology is not only a cognitive science but a moral science whose object is the social production of a docile citizenry.[11]

To grasp the extent of the constraint that Parsons has institutionalized into socialization theory we require a brief rehearsal of the main features of his social system. Simply stated the edifice is evolved from the top down. That is, it begins from a presumption of binding central consensus values and trickles down to an anticipated conformity at the level of the individual personality. When Parsons speaks of the production of a general theory of action within the system, he is addressing the persistent translation of universal cultural values into particular social norms and orientations for specific acts. Put another way, he is asking how it is that social actors routinely develop the social norms that inform their day-to-day conduct from the deeply embedded cultural sentiments at the very heart of the social system. How does the collective consciousness become real in the minds of individual people?

The acquisition of the requisite orientations for satisfactory functioning in a role is a learning process, but it is not learning in general, but a particular part of learning.

This process will be called the process of *socialization*, and the motivational processes by which it takes place, seen in terms of their functional significance to the inter- action system, the *mechanisms of socialization*. These are the mechanisms involved in the processes of 'normal' functioning of the social system.[12]

It is the social norms that provide the constraints by which the interaction between the basic dyad of Self and Other is governed (and we should note that Self and Other are referred to as Ego and Alter in the Parsonian lexicon). Thus the persistent and necessary translation of cultural values into social norms provides the dynamic within the system. Within the context of Parsons' first metaphor, it is as if the organism pulsates and its life blood circulates from the universalistic centre to the particu- laristic individual cells that constitute the mass. Social action conceived of in these terms is what Parsons refers to as 'instru- mental activism'.

The social norms become axial to the total apparatus; they are realized as both the means and the ends of all action within the system. Beyond this the social norms also provide the source of 'identity' between the individual actor and the complete system, and the overall social order itself resides in the identity between the actor and the system. The concept of 'identification' is an important one to Parsons and one that he developed from a reworking of Freud. In Freud's theory of psychosexual develop- ment the narcissistic infant was thought capable of a primitive form of object-choice, called 'identification', in which it sought an object conceived of in its own image which it therefore desired with an intensity matched only by its love for itself. In Parsons' social system the social norms are the source of this identity because they diminish the potential distinction between the self and the collectivity by engendering a coinciding set of interests for both the self and the collectivity. It is through this basic identification that individuals become committed to the social system, that they become claimed as members and, significantly, that their behaviours cohere. The social norms therefore establish the ground rules of social life and any social system achieves stability when the norms are effective in governing and maintain- ing interaction.

We should now look, in broader terms, at how the social system is constructed and how its multiple segments articulate.

At another level this will involve a moral tale of how the living body, the 'organism', is generated but how, through its functioning, it transmogrifies into a machine. In the Parsonian world it is as if life passes into death at the hands of the theorist and that the process of 'socialization' is the key to this mortification.

From the outset the system is confronted by the problem of order; however, it is simultaneously defined by Parsons in terms of that very order. At the analytic level, the social order is maintained by two pervasive system tendencies which are shared by all systems whether they are social, biological, linguistic, mathematical or whatever. These tendencies Parsons calls 'functional prerequisites' and they signify first the drive towards self-maintenance and second the drive towards boundary maintenance. These functional prerequisites refer to the inside and the outside respectively: the former to the system's capacity to sustain itself, to maintain its own equilibrium and to regulate its internal homeostatic balance; and the latter to the system's continuous capacity to pronounce its difference from other systems, to demarcate its boundaries and thus to stand in a positive and delineated relationship to its environment. We should note that these two systems do emerge primarily from bio-systems theory and they constitute the point at which the metaphors of the systemic and the organic merge and thus the point at which the rule of analysis becomes the rule of nature.

If we examine the actual framework of Parsons' social system more closely we find that it is further comprised of three distinct sub-systems. It is the functional interchange between the sub-systems which provides for both the evolution of the overall system and its emergent qualities. This functional interchange between sub-systems appears as yet another sign of life within the machine. The purposes of the sub-systems are to ensure the survival, the maintenance and the growth of the wider system. They are: the 'physical' sub-system, the 'cultural' sub-system and the 'personality' sub-system; and it is the latter which is specifically concerned with the problems of childhood and socialization.

Routinely, the personality sub-system is presented with the unsocialized child as its focus and its primary reality. The problem that the overall system is addressing here is that of sustaining existing patterns of social interaction in the wider society by invoking and awakening the latent sociality within each child. Consequently this sub-system needs to ensure that the individual child is provided with a suitable and conducive environment such that he or she will be enabled to generate the appropriate capacities that are ultimately demanded by the adult system as a whole. This complex of problems are to be handled practically by the family which acts as the locus of the child and the affective repository for the total system. The family therefore assumes a key role in Parsons' model, it is theoretically operative in successfully conducting the primary socialization of the child but it is also subsequently ascribed the duties of providing the essential emotional support of all of its members – essential, that is, in ensuring their continued functional efficiency. Socialization is clearly no meagre task. As a concept it incorporates the massive constellation of processes and accompanying paraphernalia that comprise 'person building'. In precise Parsonian terms socialization involves the lodging of the system's basic instrumental and expressive drives into the structure of individual personalities.

> We are then justified in concluding that the weight of evidence is strongly in favor of the existence and importance of an element of 'basic personality' ... which is a function of socialization in a particular type of system of role relationships with particular values. Patterns of value-orientation play a peculiarly strategic part both in the definition of role expectation patterns and in personality structure. Hence it may be concluded that it is the internalization of the value orientation patterns embodied in the role-expectations for ego of the significant socializing agents, which *constitute the strategic element of this basic personality structure.* And it is because these patterns can only be acquired through the mechanism of identification, and because the basic identification patterns are developed in childhood, that the childhood structure of personality in this respect is so stable and unchangeable.[13]

As alluded to earlier, there is a significant psychoanalytic dimension in Parsons' theorizing about the child which appears not simply through his application of certain Freudian categories but more insistently through the urgency with which he emphasizes the need to penetrate inner selves. Essentially the social system is finally dependent upon the successful capture of total personalities. This capture eclipses the possibility of individual divergence, dissolution, dissent or difference. The system is fed by the compliant personalities of its members and must, perforce, consume children.

Despite the compulsive Freudian drive in Parsons' constitution of the child there is a paradox here, namely that in a strong sense personality theory and the consequent specification of childhood emergence are not very important in his work. Parsons parades his primary commitment throughout and this is a commitment to addressing the problems relating to the stability of complex social formations. Personalities are, of course, significant here but their embodiment, namely social actors, come to be constructed in terms of the features they display that are pertinent to their functioning in the wider context, not those relevant to their difference and individuality. It is their qualities as cogs in the machine that are to be stressed. The system seeks to undermine the autonomy of the self and any subsequent expression of difference. Following from such an aspiration, Parsons' theory is characterized by a stable unitary isomorphism. This entails that all structural aspects of the social world from total social systems, through sub-systems and particular institutions down to the constitution of individual personalities, are to be viewed as formally analogous to one another. Thus personalities are microcosmically analogous to total social systems; they share the same form, content and repertoire of responses and they are similarly oriented in relation to the same universal set of choices or 'pattern variables'.

With this isomorphism in mind we can proceed to the fundamental elements of the Parsonian personality theory, which he calls 'need dispositions' and which are highly informative concerning socialization theory's conception of the child. The need dispositions display two features: first, a kind of performance or activity; and second a kind of sanction or satisfaction. Here then are the perfect ingredients for a homeostatic balance between desire and satiation. At a different level, as it is the case that all 'need dispositions' have built-in regulators, we also witness Parsonian governance at work, namely the iron hand of coercion concealed within the velvet glove of normative constraint. The essential conceptual model remains that of a naturalistic personality comprised of a battery of 'need dispositions', the gratification of which is neither wholly compatible with nor entirely possible within the personal and material limitations imposed by the social structure. Desire and constraint clash head-on and the outcome is the greater good of the collectivity. It begins to look as if we are witnessing the rebirth of the 'id' which needs to be battened-down by the 'super-ego' now emergent in the form of the social system, and this is precisely the case. The potentially overwhelming 'need dispositions', which are at the same time wholly expressive elements of the individual personality, have of necessity to be integrated, co-ordinated and modified by the value standards and role expectations extant within the system.

As with Freud's theory before, in Parsons the social bond is seen to reside in repression. The threat of infantile sexuality and the difference presented by childhood must be treated as pathological. Based on this commitment and given the integrity of a system contingent upon isomorphism the socialization process (or process of socio-libidinal castration) serves effectively to maintain both the inside and the outside within the requirements of order. That is to say that the socialization process maintains the personality system and by implication the whole social system through the very process of optimizing gratification within the limits placed by the social structure. It is a perfect regulatory mechanism; it both incorporates and contains.

To return us now to our original point, Parsons, and the powerful tradition of socialization theory that extends from his work, successfully abandons the child to the dictates of the social system. The social practice of childhood is sublimated by the theorist's presumptive motives in sustaining integration and order at the analytic level. The child, like the deviant, signifies difference. In an un-socialized state the child is manifestly profane, it threatens to bring down social worlds and the threat can only be mollified within theory by treating the child through an archetype as a proto-adult. Thus socialization theory makes sense of the child as a potential and inevitable supplicant at the altar of the corporate rationality implicit within the social system. The social practice of the child is, therefore, ultimately and necessarily displaced within the discourse of socialization. Thus Ritchie and Kollar, writing solidly within this tradition, state:

> The central concept in the sociological approach to childhood is socialization. A synonym for this process may well be acculturation because this term implies that children acquire the culture of the human groupings in which they find themselves. Children are not to be viewed as individuals fully equipped to participate in a complex

adult world, but as beings who have the potential for being slowly brought into contact with human beings.[14]

Such seemingly bland dehumanization is not uncommon within this form of reasoning. All conventional sociological worlds rest their orderliness upon a strong yet unexplicated theory of what everyone knows, that is, upon an ascriptive notion of competence on the part of their members. As a consequence of the adult member being regarded within theory as mature, rational and competent (all as natural dispositions), the child is viewed, in juxtaposition, as less than fully human, unfinished or incomplete. Such dichotomous discrimination in terms of socio-cognitive competence assumes its most explicit form in theories concerned with the learning process. It is in this context that the idea of becoming adult is taken to delineate a singular and highly specific mode of rationality. Although social theorists are aware that 'rationality' is a collective institution which addresses the relation between self and other, and despite the fact that their studies have shown them that rationality can neither dominate humankind nor be entirely free of its historical context, nevertheless, an irony persists. Within social theory particular versions of rationality are devised and manipulated in order to contrive the exclusion of certain groups. In learning theory it is the child who is so excluded.

At one level this exclusion operates within pedagogic theory and curriculum planning. The philosophy of education espoused by Hirst and Peters[15] which had teacher training in the UK in its grip for three decades provided a persuasive and, it was claimed, empirically based buttressing of such demarcation between adult and child, always at the expense of the child's interests (other than long term). So Hirst confidently asserted: 'A liberal education is, then, one that, determined in scope and content by knowledge itself, is thereby concerned with the development of mind.'[16] They elected a series of universal forms of knowledge and moral precepts for the appropriate guidance of educational practice. Their categories of understanding and their necessary maxims for the organization of knowledge all seemed to legitimate and justify existing social orders. Such an elitist ideology masquerading as disinterested analysis is entirely coherent with the non-reflexive gerontocentrism at the heart of socialization theory. Hirst and Peters and the large and influential entourage that they spawned put forward an educational programme which they described as being both 'rational' and 'liberal' in conception yet which was highly selective and thus exclusive in character. Socialization, like formal education, is a violent and painful process in the highly political sense that all people are constrained to become some categories of being rather than others. Its weakness, as theory, is to justify its constraint through a naturalistic reduction. Societies and systems of education do not have to be as they are. That they are as they are is the result of a decision.

DEVELOPMENTAL PSYCHOLOGY – THE PIAGETIAN PARADIGM

Perhaps the irony of the exclusion of the child through partial formulations of rationality is nowhere more fundamentally encountered than in the body of work known as developmental psychology. This has been defined by Piaget as follows:

> Developmental psychology can be described as the study of the development of mental functions, in as much as this development can provide an explanation, or at least a complete description, of their mechanisms in the finished state. In other words, developmental psychology consists of making use of child psychology in order to find the solution to general psychological problems.[17]

However, as Burman has pointed out:

> Nowadays the status of developmental psychology is not clear. Some say that it is a perspective or an approach to investigating general psychological problems, rather than a particular domain or sub-discipline. According to this view we can address all major areas of psychology, such as memory, cognition, etc., from this perspective. The unit of development under investigation is also variable. We could be concerned with the development of a process, or a mechanism, rather than an individual. This is in marked contrast with the popular representations of developmental psychology which equate it with the practicalities of child development or, more recently, human development.[18]

Leading within this field, and heading the 'popular representations', is the work of Piaget and his theories of intelligence and child development which have had a global impact on paediatric care and practice. Piaget's 'genetic epistemology' seeks to provide a description of the structuring of thought and finally the rational principle of nature itself, all through a theory of learning. As such Piaget's overall project represents a significant contribution to philosophy as well. Following within the neo-Kantian tradition his ideas endeavour to conciliate the divergent epistemologies of empiricism and rationalism; the former conceiving of reality as being available in the form of synthetic truths discoverable through direct experience, and the latter viewing reality analytically through the action of pure reason alone. Kant, in his time, had transcended this dichotomy through the invocation of 'synthetic *a priori* truths' that are the immanent conditions of understanding, not simply amenable to logical analysis. Piaget's categories of understanding in his scheme of conceptual development may be treated as being of the same order. His work meticulously constitutes a particular system of scientific rationality and presents it as being both natural and universal. However, as Archard stated:

> Piaget suggested that all children acquire cognitive competencies according to a universal sequence. Nevertheless, he has been criticised on two grounds. . . . First, his ideal of adult cognitive competence is a peculiarly Western philosophical one. The goal of cognitive development is an ability to think about the world with the concepts and principles of Western logic. In particular Piaget was concerned to understand how the adult human comes to acquire the Kantian categories of space, time and causality. If adult cognitive competence is conceived in this way then there is no reason to think it conforms to the everyday abilities of even Western adults. Second, children arguably possess some crucial competencies long before Piaget says they do.[19]

Piaget's empirical studies concerning the development of thought and intelligence describe, what are for him, the inevitable and clearly defined stages of intellectual growth that begin from *sensory-motor* intelligence immediately succeeding birth, and proceed through *pre-conceptual* thought, *intuitive* thought, and *concrete* operations up to the level of *formal operations*, for most people, in early adolescence. These stages are chronologically ordered but also hierarchically arranged along a continuum from low status, infantile, 'figurative' thought to high status, adult, 'operative' intelligence. This sets a narrative in the discourse of cognitive growth that is by now global and overwhelming. The 'figurative' thought that emits directly from our state of childhood, is instanced by particularistic activity, a concentration on the here and now, and a consequent inability to transfer experience or training from one situation to another. The child, for Piaget, is preoccupied with the repetitive and highly concrete replication of object states, it is clearly dominated by objective structures and inhabits a material universe. Beyond this figurative thought knows no distance or consideration, it is organized through affective responses in specific settings. Clearly we have here a recipe for 'childish-ness'.

Operative intelligence, on the other hand, the magnetic conclusion to the story, is and ought to be the province of adulthood. It implies the informed cognitive manipulation and transformation of objects by a reflecting subject. Operative intelligence is ideal, it exemplifies logical process and freedom from domination by immediate experience.

Within Piaget's system each stage of intellectual growth is characterized by a specific 'schema' or well-defined pattern and sequence of physical and mental actions governing the child's orientation to the world. Thus the system has a rhythm and a calendar too. The development and transition from figurative to operative thought, through a sequence of stages, contains an achievement ethic. That is to say that the sequencing depends upon the child's mastery and transcendence of the schemata at each stage. This implies a change in the child's relation to the world. This transition, the compulsive passage through schemata, is what Piaget refers to as a 'decentring'. The decentring of the child demonstrates a cumulative series of transformations: a change from solipsistic subjectivism to a realistic objectivity; a change from affective response to cognitive evaluation; and a movement from the disparate realm of value to the absolute realm of fact. The successful outcome of this developmental process is latterly typified and celebrated as 'scientific rationality'. This is the stage at which the child, now adult, becomes at one with the logical structure of the cosmos. At this point, where the child's matured thought provides membership of the 'circle of science' the project of 'genetic epistemology' has reached its fruition, it is complete.

However, as Venn and Walkerdine pointed out:

For Piaget, the individual subject is an exemplar, the typical representative of the species. He subscribes to the Lamarckian idea of cumulative assimilation, whereby the characteristics of individuals over time are resorbed into a single intellectual organism. Thus the processes, including those of cognitive development are the same in all single individuals, so that one need only study any exemplar and generalise.[20]

Concretely, scientific rationality for Piaget is displayed through abstraction, generalization, logico-deductive process, mathematization and cognitive operations. At the analytic level, however, this rationality reveals the intentional character of Piaget's theorizing and grounds his system in the same manner as did Parsons' transcendent 'cultural values'. Furthermore, whereas socialization through identification provided the key to the dissolution of the child within the social system, so also within Piaget's genetic epistemology, the process can be exposed as the analytic device by and through which the child is wrenched from the possibility of difference within the realm of value and integrated into the consensus that comprises the tyrannical realm of fact. Scientific rationality or adult intelligence is thus the recognition of difference grounded in unquestioned collectivity – we are returned to the irony contained within the original ontological question. The child is, once more, abandoned in theory. Real historically located children are subjected to the violence of a contemporary mode of scientific rationality which reproduces itself, at the expense of their difference, beyond the context of situated social life. Venn and Walkerdine commented further that:

> For Piaget the development of thought becomes 'indifferent to' the actual content of thought and the material base, although constructed out of it. He speaks of action on the concrete as being the basis out of which the operational structures are constructed, but his account is in the end unsatisfactory because he is more concerned with the results of abstraction as indicators of the way the mind works.[21]

The 'fact' of natural process overcomes the 'value' of real social worlds. And the normality of actual children becomes scrutinized in terms of the norms predicted by developmental psychology.

Rose, commenting on the historical context of this oppressive tendency, stated:

> Developmental psychology was made possible by the clinic and the nursery school. Such institutions had a vital role, for they enabled the observation of numbers of children of the same age, and of children of a number of different ages, by skilled psychological experts under controlled experimental, almost laboratory, conditions. Thus they simultaneously allowed for standardization and normalization – the collection of comparable information on a large number of subjects and its analysis in such a way as to construct norms. A developmental norm was a standard based upon the average abilities or performances of children of a certain age in a particular task or a specified activity. It thus not only presented a picture of what was *normal* for children of such an age, but also enabled the normality of any child to be assessed by comparison with this norm.[22]

Piaget's developmental theory states that the dynamic of the decentring process is provided by the interplay between two fundamental, complementary processes, being 'assimilation' and 'accommodation'. The two processes concern the child's choice and relation to that which is other than himself: assimilation concerns the absorption and integration of new object experiences into existing and previously organized schemata, whereas accommodation involves the modification of existing schemata, or the construction of new schemata to encapsulate new and discordant object experiences. These two processes are complementary in that accommodation generates new organizing principles with which to overcome the 'disequilibrium' produced by the new experiences that cannot be readily assimilated. Within Piaget's demonstrations of adult scientific rationality, the child is deemed to have appropriately adapted to the environment when he or she has achieved a balance between accommodation and assimilation. It would seem that the juggling with homeostasis is forever the child's burden! However, although from a critical analytic stance accommodation might be regarded as the source of the child's integration into the consensus reality, within the parameters of the original theory the process is treated as the locus of creativity and innovation – it is that aspect of the structuring of thought and being which is to be most highly valued. In contradistinction Piaget regards children's play as non-serious, trivial activity in as much as it displays an emphasis on assimilation over accommodation. Play is merely diverting fun or fantasy, it deflects the child from his true destiny and logical purpose within the scheme of rationality. The problem is that the criteria for what constitutes play need not equate with the rigorous, factual, demands of reality. Treating play in this manner, that is from the perspective of the rational and 'serious' adult, Piaget is specifically undervaluing what might represent an important aspect of the expressive practices of the child and his or her world. Following the work of Denzin:

> Childhood is conventionally seen as a time of carefree, disorganised bliss. . . . The belief goes that they [children] enjoy non-serious, play-directed activities. They avoid work and serious activities at all costs. . . . There is a paradox in these assumptions.[23]

And Stone:

> Educators too often have a restricted view of play, exercise, and sport, asking only how such activities contribute to the motor efficiency and longevity of the organism. Yet the symbolic significance of recreation is enormous, providing a fundamental bond that ties the individual to his society. . . . Social psychologists have long recognised the significance of play for preparing young children to participate later on in adult society.[24]

In this context I would argue that play is indeed an important component of the child's work as a social member. And I would argue further that play is instrumental in what Speier[25] has designated the child's 'acquisition of interactional competencies'. Genetic epistemology wilfully disregards, or perhaps just pays insufficient attention to, play in its urge to mathematize and thus render formal the 'rational' cognitive practices of adult individuals in their collective lives.

By treating the growth process of the child's cognition as if it were impelled towards a prestated structure of adult rationality, Piaget is driven to concur with Lévi-Bruhl's concept of the 'primitive mentality' of the savage, but in this instance in relation to the 'pre-logical' thought of the child. A further consequence of Piaget's conceptualization of the rational development of the child's 'embryonic' mind as if it were a natural process, is that the critical part played by language in the articulation of mind and self is very much understated. Language is treated as a symbolic vehicle which carries thought and assists in the growth of concepts and a semiotic system, but it is not regarded as having a life in excess of these referential functions. Thus language, for Piaget, is insufficient in itself to bring about the mental operations which make concept formation possible. Language, then, helps in the selection, storage and retrieval of information but it does not bring about the co-ordination of mental operations. This level of organization is conceptualized as taking place above language and in the domain of action. This is slightly confusing until we realize that action, for Piaget, is not regarded as the performative conduct that generates social contexts, but rather as a sense of behaviour that is rationally governed within the *a priori* strictures of an idealist metaphysics. Language, for Piaget, itemizes the world and acts as a purely cognitive function. This is a position demonstrably confounded by Merleau-Ponty in his work on the existential and experiential generation and use of language by children – the classic example being the child's generation of a past tense in order to express the loss of uniqueness and total parental regard following the birth of a sibling; language here is not naming a state of affairs but expressing the emotion of jealousy. Merleau-Ponty's work serves to reunite the cognitive and the affective aspects of being which are so successfully sundered by Piaget. He stated:

> I pass to the fact that appeared to me to be worthy of mention . . . the relation that can be established between the development of intelligence (in particular, the acquisition of language) and the configuration of the individual's affective environment.[26]

At the outset of this chapter I commented on the absence of any consensus view of the child within social theory. This is, perhaps, no bad thing. I have attempted to explicate certain of the normative assumptions at the heart of 'socialization theory' and 'developmental psychology' which have held as the orthodoxy up until recent years and I might optimistically suggest that such conventional explanations have been successfully supplanted by feminist theories in relation to the family and what have come to be grouped as 'social constructionist' views of the child, possibly instigated by this author but subsequently titled and joined by significant company.[27] However, a spurious consensus is not necessarily a desirable goal. It has been my intention to show that it is the different manners in which theoretical commitments are grounded that gives rise to the diversity of views of childhood.

My critical appraisals of Parsons and Piaget were not random selections. They have been singled out for analysis because of the clarity and penetration of their work, but more significantly because of the immense influence that they have exercised on the social sciences in the areas of socialization theory and learning theory. Extending beyond this both theorists, but particularly Piaget, have had an immeasurable impact upon the everyday common-sense conceptualization of the child. They and the paradigms that they have established have, to a large extent, captured and monopolized the child in social theory and in so doing have exemplified the point of this chapter. The idea of childhood is not a natural but a social construct and as such its status is constituted in particular socially located forms of discourse. Whether the child is being considered in the common-sense world or in the disciplined world of specialisms, the meaningfulness of the child as a social being derives from its place and its purpose in theory. Social theory is not merely descriptive and certainly never disinterested. In the variety of approaches that social theory adopts in relation to the child there is an analytic gathering around my central theme in this chapter, namely, that the child is constituted purposively within such theory. That is, the child is assembled intentionally to serve the purposes of supporting and perpetuating the fundamental grounds of and versions of humankind, action, order, language and rationality within particular theories. We are thus presented with different 'theoretical' children who serve the different theoretical models of social life from which they spring. The point is a phenomenological one.

My recommendation remains then, that a sociology of childhood should arise from the constitutive practices that provide for the child and the child–adult relationship. Any potential theorist of childhood who wishes to engage in such an analysis, as I have attempted with 'socialization theory' and 'developmental psychology', should realize that they too are responsible for constituting the child, and that different images and representations of the child are occasioned by the different theoretic social worlds that we inhabit. In this way the passage of our theorizing will continue to emerge from the stenosis of the dominant 'natural' archetypes of childhood, being those of either the pathological or the schismatic. We need no longer abandon the child either to ignorance and secondary status or to radical difference and a bipartite world.

Let us now, in the following chapter, explore some of the constraints placed upon a sociological conception of the child.

NOTES

[1] H. Cunningham, *The Children of the Poor: Representations of Childhood since the Seventeenth Century*, Oxford: Blackwell, 1991, p. 6.

[2] J. Hillman, *Loose Ends*, Irving (Texas): Spring Publications, 1975, p. 8.

[3] M. Speier, 'The everyday world of the child' in J. Douglas (ed.), *Understanding Everyday Life*, London: Routledge & Kegan Paul, 1970, p. 188.

[4] J. O'Neill, 'Embodiment and child development: a phenomenological approach' in H. P. Dreitzel (ed.), *Recent Sociology No. 5*, New York: Collier Books, 1973, p. 65.

[5] B. Bernstein, 'On the classification and framing of educational knowledge' in M. F. D. Young (ed.), *Knowledge and Control*, London: Collier-Macmillan, 1972, p. 47.

[6] P. Coveney, *The Image of Childhood*, Harmondsworth: Penguin, 1967, p. 29.

[7] I. Opie and P. Opie, *The Lore and Language of Schoolchildren*, Oxford: Oxford University Press, 1959.

[8] See F. Elkin and G. Handel, *The Child and Society: The Process of Socialization*, New York: Random House, 1972; N. Denzin, *Childhood Socialization*, San Francisco: Jossey-Bass, 1977; D. Goslin (ed.), *Handbook of Socialization Theory and Research*, Chicago: Rand McNally, 1969; K. Danziger (ed.), *Readings in Child Socialization*, Oxford: Pergamon; A. Morrison and D. McIntyre, *Schools and Socialization*, Harmondsworth: Penguin, 1971; G. White, *Socialization*, London: Longman, 1977.

[9] D. Wrong, 'The oversocialized conception of man in modern sociology' in *American Sociological Review*, XXVI, April 1961, p. 190.

[10] T. Parsons, *The Social System*, London: Routledge & Kegan Paul, 1951, p. 207.

[11] J. O'Neill, *The Poverty of Postmodernism*, London: Routledge, 1994, pp. 26–27.

[12] T. Parsons, op. cit., p. 205.

[13] Ibid., p. 228.
[14] O. W. Ritchie and M. R. Kollar, *The Sociology of Childhood*, New York: Appleton-Century-Crofts, 1964, p. 24.
[15] P. H. Hirst and R. S. Peters, *The Logic of Education*, London: Routledge & Kegan Paul, 1970; R. S. Peters, *Ethics and Education*, London: Allen & Unwin, 1966; R. F. Deardon, P. H. Hirst and R. S. Peters (eds), *Education and the Development of Reason*, London: Routledge & Kegan Paul, 1972; P. H. Hirst, *Knowledge and the Curriculum*, London: Routledge & Kegan Paul, 1972.
[16] P. H. Hirst, op. cit., p. 72.
[17] J. Piaget, *Psychology and Epistemology* (trans. P. Wells), Harmondsworth: Penguin, 1972, p. 32.
[18] E. Burman, *Deconstructing Developmental Psychology*, London: Routledge, 1994, p. 9.
[19] D. Archard, *Children: Rights and Childhood*, London: Routledge, 1993, pp. 65–66.
[20] C. Venn and V. Walkerdine, 'The acquisition and production of knowledge: Piaget's theory reconsidered' in *Ideology and Consciousness*, no. 3, 1978, p. 79.
[21] Ibid., p. 87.
[22] N. Rose, *Governing the Soul*, London: Routledge, 1990, p. 142.
[23] N. Denzin, 'The work of little children' in C. Jenks (ed.), *The Sociology of Childhood*, London: Batsford, 1982 (and Aldershot: Gregg, 1992, p. 189).
[24] G. Stone, 'The play of little children' in *Quest* 4, Human Kinetic Publishers, 1965, p. 23.
[25] M. Speier, op. cit.
[26] M. Merleau-Ponty, *The Primacy of Perception*, Chicago: Northwestern University Press, 1964, p. 108.
[27] C. Jenks, 1982, op. cit. See also A. James and A. Prout (eds), *Constructing and Reconstructing Childhood*, Basingstoke: Falmer, 1990; J. Qvortrup, *Childhood as a Social Phenomenon*, Vienna: The European Centre, 1993; W. Stainton Rogers, H. Hevey and E. Ash (eds), *Child Abuse and Neglect*, London: Batsford, 1989.

2

The conceptual limitations on a sociological approach to childhood

In this chapter I shall not address the child as a practical and pre-stated being and then offer advice concerning its appropriate mode of maturation in the manner of developmental psychology or paediatrics. Rather I attempt here to realize the child as constituted socially, as a status of person which is comprised through a series of, often heterogeneous, images, representations, codes and constructs. This is an increasingly popular perspective within contemporary childhood studies.[1]

Such an approach, in this context, displays a variety of purpose: first, an endeavour to displace the overwhelming claim on childhood from the realm of common-sense reasoning – not that such reasoning is inferior or unsystematic, but that it is conventional rather than disciplined,[2] it serves to 'naturalize' the child in each and any epoch and thus to disenable our understanding of the child within a particular historical context. Children, quite simply, are not always the same thing. Second, the approach indicates that the child, like other forms of being within our culture, is made present through a variety of forms of discourse. These are not necessarily competitive but neither is their complementarity inherent and a holistic view of the child does not arise from a liberal sense of varieties of interpretation or multiple realities. Rather, the identity of children or of a particular child varies within the political contexts of those forms of discourse – hence, the different kinds of 'knowledge' of mother, teacher, paediatrician, social worker, educational psychologist and juvenile magistrate, for example, do not live suspended in an egalitarian harmony. Hendrick,[3] in this context, has produced an instructive account of childhood constructions in Britain since 1800 through the analysis of a series of dominant forms of discourse, in which he includes the 'romantic', the 'evangelical', the 'factory', the 'delinquent', the 'schooled', the 'psycho-medical, the 'welfare', the 'psychological' and the 'family' as opposed to the 'public' child – these languages have all provided for different modern lives of children. As Hendrick himself stated: 'My hope is that a familiarity with these perceptions, as held by dominant interests within our society, will help to explain both the tenacity and the self-confidence of western interpretations of childhood.'[4] Third, the approach intends to work out the parameters within which sociology, and thus its relation to understanding childhood, must originate – therefore I attempt to show sociology's conceptual limitations, and also its possibilities, as one form of discourse about the world. It is with this last point that I begin.

STRUCTURAL CAUSALITY

Although, in its various guises, sociology emerged as a critical response to the state of its culture and traditionally adopted a radical position in relation to the material constraints wrought through the progress of modernity, it was also, in origin, epistemologically imperialistic. Comte,[5] a founding figure, specified that human knowledge, at both the societal and individual level, would inevitably develop through three stages, the theological, the metaphysical and the positive – the latter designated science, and the supreme and most synthetic form of this activity was to be sociology itself; it would supersede all other forms of knowing – it would become the 'queen of sciences'. Thompson summarized this well:

> The Law of Three Stages stated that each branch of knowledge passes successively through three different theoretical conditions: the theological or fictitious; the metaphysical or abstract; and the scientific or positive. In

the theological state the human mind searches for the
origin and purpose of all effects and supposes that all
phenomena are produced by the immediate action of
supernatural beings. In the metaphysical state the mind
supposes that abstract forces (personified abstractions,
actual entities) produce all phenomena. In the final stage,
the positive stage, the mind gives up the vain search for
absolute notions, the origin and destination of the universe, and the causes of phenomena, and studies their
laws, that is, their relations of succession and resemblance.[6]

Durkheim,[7] Comte's successor, extended this project by delin-
eating sociology's peculiar realm of phenomena. He marked out
their identifiable characteristics and the conceptual space that
they occupied and he sought to devalue all other attempts to
explain 'social' reality.[8] Thus we arrive at a kernel idea for sociology, that of the 'social structure'; it is from this concept that
the discipline proceeds. Social structures appear to societal members as 'facts' and as such have real and describable characteristics: they are typical, that is, they are a series of normal or
taken-for-granted manifestations; further, they are constraining
upon the actions of members either implicitly or explicitly; and
finally they are, to some greater or lesser degree, independent of
their individual will. Social structures are 'facts', they are real,
and they are real in their consequences for human action. As
Durkheim put it himself:

The proposition which states that social facts must be
treated as things – the proposition which is at the very
basis of our method – is among those which have stirred
up the most opposition. It was deemed paradoxical and
scandalous for us to assimilate to the realities of the
external world the realities of the social world. This was
singularly to misunderstand the meaning and effect of
this assimilation, the object of which was not to reduce
the higher forms of being to the level of lower ones but,
on the contrary, to claim for the former a degree of
reality at least equal to that which everyone accords the
latter. Indeed, we do not say that social facts are material
things, but that they are things just as are material things,
although in a different way.[9]

The 'social structure' then becomes the supra-individual source of causality in sociological explanations whether it is experienced by members as a cognitive, moral, political or economic orientation.[10] All sociological worlds seek to build in and analyse a series of constraints that work upon the individual and however the particular perspective places itself within the debate over free will versus determinism there tends to be a primary commitment to treat the self as an epiphenomenon of the society[11] and thus prey to apprehension in terms of epistemological binaries. As O'Neill put it:

> The *tabula rasa* or clean-slate individual of liberal contract theory is as much a fiction as is its counterpart fiction of the many-headed monster state, or Leviathan. Each device serves to stampede thought into those forced alternatives of the under- or over-socialized individual.[12]

Sociology's tradition then makes little claim to provide a strong theory of the individual and this holds implications for our understanding of the child. Ironically, the most contemporary sociology of the late- or post-modern scene is even less secure in its explanations of self.[13] Thus despite the apparent cult of the individual and celebration of the ego in the latter part of the twentieth century, sociological analysis appears increasingly unprepared to formulate the social identity of people, let alone the emergent identity of children.

The problems of structural causality, in relation to a study of the child, are further compounded by the fact that sociological systems of explanation are constructed in relation to the conduct of typical rational 'adult' members – children are largely theorized as states of pathology or inadequacy in relation to the pre-stated model of the actor as was discussed at length in the previous chapter. All sociologies, in their variety of forms, relate to the childhood experience through theories of socialization, whether in relation to the institutional contexts of the family, the peer group or the school. These three sites are regarded as the serious arenas wherein the child is most systematically exposed to concerted induction procedures. It is here that the child, within the social system, relates as a subordinate to the formalized strategies of constraint, control, inculcation and patterning which will serve to transform his or her status into the tangible and intelligible form of an adult competent being.

> In sociological writings characterized as normative, the
> term socialization glosses the phenomenon of change
> from the birth of a child to maturity or old age. To
> observe that changes take place after birth is trivial, but
> the quasiscientific use of the term socialization masks this
> triviality. In fact, the study of these changes as socializ-
> ation is an expression of the sociologists' common sense
> position in the world – i.e., as adults. The notion of
> socialization leads to the theoretical formulations mirror-
> ing the adult view that children are incomplete adults.[14]

A child's social, and ontological, purpose is therefore, it would
seem, not to stay a child. Within this inexorable trajectory any
signs of entrenchment or backtracking, like play for example,
may be interpreted as indicators of a failure to 'develop' – an
imperative that supports the practice of much educational psychology, as we saw in the previous chapter.[15]

It is a further irony that were one to confront a sociologist
with the issue of 'development' then their immediate frame of
reference would be to consider the modes of transition occurring
between the structures of simple and complex societies.[16] The
concept of development, with relation to persons, is no part of a
sociologist's vocabulary. Structures are sociologists' primary
realities and the only organism that they might consider in a state
of development is that, by analogy, of the society as a whole.
However, to depict sociology's tradition in this way is not to
simply indicate closure. To understand the parameters of our
discipline is to understand our disposition towards the world –
we may now seek to address child development with a reflexive
attention to the origins of our form of speech.[17]

THE CONCEPT OF DEVELOPMENT – TIME, NATURE
AND PROGRESS

'Development', an essentially temporal notion, is the primary
metaphor through which childhood is made intelligible, both in
the everyday world and also within the specialist vocabularies
of the sciences and agencies which lay claim to an understanding
and servicing of that state of being. Thus, stemming from this
root metaphor all empirical study, social policy, or remedial treatment in relation to the child tends to be longitudinal in character

– the idea of time being left inviolable. James and Prout are in agreement over this point:

> The social construction of time in and through social relationships is a relatively neglected theoretical theme within contemporary sociology. In recent years, however, there has been a re-awakening of interest in the temporal dimension of social relationships and ... we will take up the invitation implicit in such work to suggest that the social construction of time may be crucial to the study of childhood. Such a move is important, we suggest, in facilitating a wider and more critical thinking about childhood as a social institution and about the lives of children themselves.[18]

Given 'time' the child will change. More than this, development as the all-pervading source of the location of the child-as-other, has come to be realized as a wholly 'natural' process in a manner that more than echoes the determinism of sociology's structural bias. Individuals are largely understood to be realizations of what was bio-genetically inherent, with perhaps a surface structure of personality, thought-style or cognitive breadth being attributable to 'nurture' – though even these finite provinces have been invaded by certain theories which sought to explain criminality, racial deficit or insanity.[19] Finally, development has certain resonances within the culture of modernity that enable the idea to be conflated with other axial contemporary social metaphors like 'growth' and 'progress'. Within a post-Darwinian framework we are led to relate to development as necessary, inevitable and, essentially, for the good.

Let us now address these central elements in the concept of development. First, in relation to the issue of development as time, philosophers from Plato to the present day have grappled with the indeterminacy or experiential character of this dimension, yet most modern thinking appears locked within a Kantian sense of time as both external and quantitative.[20] This in itself is a sociologically interesting phenomenon bound up with the scientism and mathematizing urge of contemporary society. However, what such mechanical diachronicity constrains and disfigures is the actual experience of time in social relations, as Durkheim asserted: 'A calendar expresses the rhythm of the collective activities, while at the same time its function is to assure their regularity.'[21] In everyday social life we are quite accustomed to the variability of the 'time' experience; time spent with a lover is not comparable to time spent queuing in the supermarket. In similar fashion the existential experience of being a child seems to go on forever, the gap between Christmases seems unimaginable, bedtime is all too suddenly here and 'boring' time, doing usually what parents want to do, is interminable.

> Unlike adults who have learned to anticipate the future and thus manage delay, children have a built-in time sense based on the urgency of their instinctual and emotional needs. As an infant's memory begins to incorporate the way in which parents satisfy wishes and needs, as well as the experience of the reappearance of parents after their disappearance, a child gradually develops the capacity to delay gratification and to anticipate and plan for the future.[22]

Parallel with such interior sensation for the child parents are unified in their sense that children 'grow up so quickly' and are no sooner walking than they are asking to borrow the car!

Second, the 'naturalizing' of development can be seen to obscure or mystify a set of criteria for change which might be implicit or grounded within a specific network of interests. Thus as examples, to have one's child designated as 'advanced' in relation to Piagetian criteria may be a source of pride to a parent as it signifies rapid or special 'natural' development; the criteria for such 'development' remain, however, normative and unexplicated – the same parent might experience acute displeasure if their child were defined as 'retarded' and thus relegated to an educational identity of a lesser status; the same covert criteria apply. It is often argued that natal induction, viewed as a critical stage of 'development', is necessary for the benefit of the child but it would seem, in many cases, to relate wholly to the politics of hospital timetables. Clearly the increased availability of the voluntary termination of pregnancies relates to the politics of maternal autonomy and to no part of a 'natural' developmental cycle. We can explore further contemporary examples within the spectrum of child development: in 1978 in the United Kingdom, the Warnock Committee[23] reported on children with 'special needs' and advised that at any one time one-third of the total school population would have special needs, but that this one-third is not a fixed group; from which one may deduce that the 'natural' pattern of development of each and every child potentially consists of 'needs', 'disadvantages' or 'handicaps', but only in relation to the provisions of the existing educational system. Finally, we may attend to the moral panic and media focus that surrounded the supposed startling outbreak of cases of 'child abuse' within the Cleveland Health Authority in the United Kingdom during 1987. So extensive was the proportion of reported and estimated cases within that total population that one may be led to suppose that child abuse was not a pathological form of social relation, but indeed part of the 'natural' cycle of development of most children (a bizarre and deliberately ironic argument that would be given some weight with historical evidence).[24] These examples are cited to demonstrate the utterly 'social' and embedded character of the 'natural' experience of childhood.

Third, the conflation of development with ideas of growth and progress builds a competitive ethic into the process of development itself which supports the ideology of possessive individualism at the root of industrialized capitalist cultural formations. The dominant materialist reduction functions such that not only are mental and manual skills evaluated hierarchically and therefore stratified which, in turn, enables social stratification within the culture, but also manual/physical development is itself realized as internally competitive to generate further modes of stratification and ranking. There would appear to be a justified merit that stems from development. Such processes extend from the comparative parental talk at ante-natal clinics, such as 'Is he crawling yet?', 'When did she start to walk?', 'Mine could talk at that age', to the pinnacles of nationalistic projections in the form of the Olympic Games with collective physical prowess being measured by medal counts (and backward countries sometimes surprising advanced nations with their physical precocity). After all, success should accompany development – naturally!

What I am suggesting is that the concept of development does not signify a 'natural' process – it does, however, make reference to a socially constructed sense of change pertaining to the young individual which is encoded within a series of benchmarks relevant to the topical or predominant form of discourse: which can relate to political engagement, moral and criminal responsibility, sexual consent and patterns of consumption. Thus different codes move in and out of focus according to which aspect of the person we are attending to – in many senses there is a heterogeneity to these codes which resists the attempts to reduce them to the homogeneity of 'naturalness'.

The positive side of this deconstruction of the child experience into an assembly of signifying discourses is to explore certain possibilities within the social character of that encoding. While regarding childhood phenomenologically, in terms of the intentional constitutive practices that facilitate its recognizable form, it is not necessary to pursue such a tradition to the point of the child being wholly disembodied – as Merleau-Ponty and O'Neill[25] have both, separately, argued – to do so deprives the child of an ontology.

A crucial aspect of childhood, and a sociological sense of 'development', can be realized in terms of its 'contingency'. That is to say that childhood always speaks of a relationship, e.g. adult–child, parent–child, teacher–child, etc.[26] As Ambert put it:

> The discussion is informed by a critical perspective viewing both childhood and parenting as social constructs that evolve with sociohistorical changes . . . discussion of parenting cannot be divorced from perspectives on the nature of childhood . . . the nature of childhood is fluid, anchored as it is in the prevailing world views supporting societies and created by societies. In most societies, children and early adolescents are viewed within the context of the family. Consequently, as one cohort or one culture defines what childhood is, parenting is constructed, whether implicitly or explicitly.[27]

Also, whatever the general condition of childhood in society (treated violently, exploited, pornographized) it may be regarded as an index of the state of the wider social relation, the moral bond in society.[28]

The concept of development, then, might imply that the child's 'becoming' is dependent upon the reference points or normative structures made conventional within the adults' world, but we need to pursue this idea further. In the obvious, cultural sense of the attribution, ascription and assumption of meaning, all people 'need' others in order to generate a meaningful environment for change, stasis or whatever; quite simply, we cannot make sense alone. Any knowledge of self derives from an experience of collective constraint; and being and action, as opposed to being and behaviour, is contingent upon the presence of and communication with others. Adults, however, are assumed within social theory to operate with a degree of basic reciprocity of perspectives and interchangeability of standpoints in terms of the processes of meaning giving and meaning receiving.[29] On top of this, adult relationships are subsequently stratified in terms of an unequal distribution of power.

The difference that is childhood may well be understood in terms of power,[30] though this would be to treat the grounds of power as purely age-based (in the same way that Marxist feminism attempted to reduce the question of power to an issue of gender), neither argument is adequate nor sufficient. However, childhood might be more instructively theorized in terms of dependency. Children do practically have 'need' of their parents and adult companions, a need that is a combination of the material, physical, emotional and so on, but one that is always realized within particular socio-historical, and cultural, settings. This understanding enables us to look towards the contexts of provision, instruction and care in relation to a fundamental sociological analytic concept, that of 'altruism'. Thus the child–adult relation is, in one sense, expressive of 'altruism', a dimension of sociality that is at odds with the dominant image of self and success within modernity, namely the ascendance of egoism.[31] Perhaps, therefore, we should express the child–adult relation in multi-dimensional terms. As Gilligan has stated:

> The different parameters of the parent–child relationship
> – its inequality and its interdependence or attachment
> – may ground different feelings which differentiate the
> dimension of inequality/equality and attachment/detach-
> ment that characterize all forms of human connection. In
> contrast to a unitary moral vision and to the assumption
> that the opposite of the one is the many, these two dimen-
> sions of relationship provide coordinates for reimagining
> the self and remapping development. The two concep-
> tions of responsibility, reflecting different images of the
> self in relationship, correct an individualism that has been
> centred within a single interpretive framework.[32]

But I am not arguing that the altruism or care that the adult feels towards the child is itself a unitary or a 'natural' feeling – no, rather I would suggest that it is a social construct. In one sense this construct might be viewed as the embodiment of the affective myth of romanticism that has given rise to the modern nuclear family, and perhaps we should add the 'mother', as the centre of all loving sensations – the instrumental accompaniment to the exaggeration and elevation of the autonomous cognitive ego that has followed in the wake of the Enlightenment and assisted in the growth of science and capitalism.[33] In fact, a feature of its time, no more and no less. Again Ambert was instructive in this context when she stated that:

> This linkage between what we conceive to be the nature of childhood and that of parenting is based less on the natural unavoidability of parents for children's survival and well-being as on society's structure and socio-economic requisites, which not only place children in the context of family, but 'parentalize' and, I will add, 'maternalize' them. Thus, when one sees children, one 'sees' parents. When one sees children who have problems, one looks for parents, especially mothers.[34]

The sociological tradition would, however, attest to altruism as the very core of sociality. All sociologies spring from the Hobbesian problem of order and even if they attend to the conflictual character of social relations their basic commitment is to explain how societies hold together. In this latter sense altruism may be read as ideological, an appearance of care that disguises the true purpose of control. Here the social sense of dependency that accompanies development takes on a sinister form, we have to shake ourselves free of the warm sense of sociality that holds together through spontaneous loving bonds. We are then confronted with a more cynical version of the idea, and the mechanisms of dependence that serve to sustain particular versions of the status quo are revealed. In this sense the development of the child may now instructively be viewed alongside the development of the Afro-American in the USA or the Black South African, or indeed, the development of women's consciousness in Western Europe. Care, in this sense, itself becomes hegemonic,[35] it provides a moral and philosophical context for social relations which claims the assent of large groups of the people for a sustained period. Care becomes part of a subtle ideology that possesses the moral high ground, defies opposition and exercises a continual control over the other in the name of 'what is best for them'. Following from this dependence is realized as that feature of social structures which seeks to individualize guilt, pathologize the individual and which further militates to disguise the failures or shortcomings implicit within those very social structures. To this extent all societies demonstrate 'dependence' through their members' adherence to drink, drugs, belief systems or desires.

Instead of asking 'Why is my child a heroin addict, what went wrong in his or her development?' we should, from a sociological perspective, be asking 'What is it about this free, liberal, advanced, technological democracy that makes heroin a desirable alternative possible course of action?' Development through dependency then becomes an instrument in the processes of social and cultural reproduction.[36]

THE CHILD IN CRITICAL SOCIAL THEORY

Let us now look at certain aspects of the critical mode of social theorizing within sociology that would most systematically espouse this view. Althusser[37] divides the mechanisms of control in modern societies into two forms, the Repressive and the Ideological State Apparatuses. The latter contains all aspects of superstructure, the cognitive and transmissional aspects of culture, which serve to reproduce the existing oppressive structures of power and advantage without exposing naked aggression. Thus family life, patterns of socialization, schooling – all complementary contexts of a child's development, are realized as part of the deep structurally unconscious apparatuses whereby the going order is recharged, reaffirmed and reconstituted. The education system, Althusser told us:

> takes children from every class at infant school and then for years ... it drums into them ... a certain amount of know-how wrapped up in the ruling ideology or simply the ruling ideology in its pure state. Each mass ejected en route is practically provided with the ideology which suits the role it has to fulfil in class society: the role of exploited, of the agent of repression or of the professional ideologist.[38]

Marcuse[39] has attended to the contemporary liberal *laissez-faire* adjustment to, and understanding of, the behaviour of others which we can clearly relate to the socialization process that he regards as a 'repressive tolerance'. It might be likened to a cultural mannerism of acceptance that defuses critique, reaction or change through its all-pervading quasi-approval. In an efficient, 'caring' society child-rearing and education liberate the individual into compliance. Marcuse stated that 'A comfortable, smooth, reasonable, democratic unfreedom prevails in advanced industrial civilization, a token of technical progress',[40] and sadly concluded that:

> To liberate the imagination so that it can be given all its means of expression presupposes the repression of much that is now free and that perpetuates a repressive society. And such reversal is not a matter of psychology or ethics but of politics . . . [that is] the practice in which the basic societal institutions are developed, defined, sustained, and changed. It is the practice of individuals no matter how organized they may be. Thus the question once again must be faced: how can the administered individuals – who have made their mutilation into their own liberties and satisfactions, and thus reproduced it on an enlarged scale – liberate themselves from themselves as well as from their masters?[41]

This is an utterance redolent with critique of the contemporary adult–child relationship.

Bourdieu and Passeron,[42] whose work specifically addresses the process of social reproduction, demonstrated that there are intellectual fields of appraisal which surround any creative endeavour or unique form of expression and both render it meaningful and evaluate it in relation to existing patterns of social stratification. This can apply to the work of art but equally well to the performance of the developing child in significant social contexts like schools. Children, they argue, are differentially endowed with a 'cultural capital' according to their original social milieu, their 'habitus'.

> It may be assumed that every individual owes to the type of schooling he has received a set of basic, deeply interiorised master-patterns on the basis of which he subsequently acquires other patterns, so that the system of patterns by which his thought is organised owes its specific character not only to the nature of the patterns constituting it but also to the frequency with which these are used and to the level of consciousness at which they operate, these properties being probably connected with the circumstances in which the most fundamental intellectual patterns were acquired.[43]

They are equipped with thought styles, manners, sensitivities and patterns of relevance and relation that ensure a re-production of their class position and the ideological framework that supports such a locus. Societies, it would seem, almost inevitably reproduce their structures of hierarchy and power through the processes of the development of self: 'education serves to transform the cultural heritage into a common individual unconscious'.[44]

Finally, the work of Foucault,[45] which we shall examine in more detail in the following chapter, offers us, at one level, a series of archaeologies of the strategies of control and oppression that have been exercised within modern western culture. Thus when he informs us of the change and development in penology in Western Europe we find a historical transition from the excessive, explicit symbolic punishment of the seventeenth century to a gradually more subtle, implicit and intrusive mode of discipline embodied in its finest modern form in Bentham's 'panopticon' – the dream building, the rational correction machine. In this form, which we may parallel with the development of modern techniques of child-rearing, absolute surveillance is the key. The developing individual, either within the context of criminal punishment or that of education, is to be watched, monitored, timetabled, regimented and exposed. The private becomes more and more available to the public. Bodies and minds claim an allegiance to the social through dependency, guilt and visibility.

Emerging from a different sociological perspective to the above, the work of Bernstein[46] has, for over two decades, provided a major source of inspiration for theory and research concerning child-rearing, child development and educational disadvantage. While apparently leaving the grounds of moral consensus within society intact he addresses the causes of differential educational achievement within the population of developing children. He was among the first to sophisticate the 'educability' thesis beyond an explanation of child performance in relation to their particular constellations of positively or negatively oriented structural variables. Bernstein does not ignore the effect of social factors on a child's development but he shows how they become realized as world views and thus courses of action – in this sense he reveals his true concern as being not with the issue of educability but rather with the complex relation between the social structure and the symbolic order. His central question is: 'How does our outside environment become transformed into modes of consciousness?' and this clearly provides a potentially dialectical view of development. Bernstein's analysis moves from the level of different types of community structure, through parental control variants, on to the linguistic realization of unique intent. Social stratification, however, remains the dominant implicit dimension. We shall hear more of Bernstein's work in the next chapter.

CHILDHOOD AS CONSTRAINT

What this brief summary of sociological theory relevant to child development aims at is not a summation of the central insights, all of which have been injured by the brevity of my exposition, but rather to show that even that large section of the discipline which is clearly critical of any existing form of social relations and thus dedicated to its change, even this body of work, seems unable to mobilize the potentiality of the child as an agent of such change. The development of the child seems variously articulated as a process of entrapment. The newness and difference of childhood faces standardization and normalization. Thus, to return to the earlier theme of this chapter, all social influences on the developing child are presented and understood as structural constraints.

During the 1960s in the United Kingdom – a time of full employment, economic expansion, growth in public provision and a liberalizing of previously entrenched attitudes towards human behaviour – education became viewed by government and populace alike as a crucial investment in the future collective good. The dominant ideology contained a strong sense of 'human capital' that eventually blossomed into the 'vocationalism' of the late 1980s and the 1990s. Schooling and university education expanded considerably and efforts were also made to improve its quality. This general attitude of the collective consciousness was reflected within sociology where the sociology of education became a burgeoning specialism. However, even within such a climate of progressive optimism the primary thesis was that, if ability is randomly distributed, how is it that educational achievement is socially distributed? Sociologists produced a plethora of studies which offered explanation in terms of such variables as family size, parental occupation, parental income, achievement motivation, immediate versus deferred gratification, peer group orientation, cultural deprivation, language use and complexes of these.[47] Again, all of these variables were reducible to indices of social class, but more significantly at an analytic level, all are intelligible as contexts of non-wilfulness. Even social theory that is critical seems to depotentiate the young through an intrinsically pessimistic vision. The developing social actors, who are 'the developing child', are rendered passive receivers and perpetuators of the accidents of their historical moment. This is perhaps best epitomized in the irony of a study by Willis[48] when he states that the reason that working-class children succumb to social and cultural reproduction is because they are complicit in the processes, they are effectively active agents in their own lack of mobility.

> The difficult thing to explain about how middle class kids get middle class jobs is why the others let them. The difficult thing to explain about how working class kids get working class jobs is why they let themselves.
> It is much too facile simply to say that they have no choice.... There is no obvious physical coercion and a degree of self direction.[49]

It would seem then that the social factors affecting development are such that they become internalized and expressed as matters of choice!

Development conceived of in these terms speaks not of an unfolding, a project of creativity and inspiration, in fact hardly of the individual child's biography at all. The child continues to be realized as an instance of a category and the concept of development only ever seems to depict the concerted and ultimately omnipotent violence of the social structure to which the individual inevitably succumbs. This is not to argue for the mobilization of the concrete child as a political force in response to these actual constraints as part of a 'children's rights' movement, but rather to argue analytically for a more radical conception of the child as a vision and as a potential.

Development, though a dominant image in understanding the child, is only one way. Further, as this chapter has attempted to demonstrate, it is that kind of concept which encourages the stance of looking backwards from within the sociological tradition. But sociology and its address of the child can occupy different spaces; let us take three possible examples. First, the child might be regarded historically, not as a series of evolutionary steps, but rather as a patterning of images that relate to different temporal contexts. In this way Ariès,[50] the leading figure in a school of neo-Enlightenment historians whose ideas we shall explore in more detail later, looks at visual representations and fashion and shows the emergence of childhood within a particular group and within a particular epoch. Others have looked, for example, to a gendered history of childhood:

> After the fourteenth century, with the development of the bourgeoisie and empirical science, this situation slowly began to evolve. The concept of childhood developed as an adjunct to the modern family ... 'childrenese' became fashionable during the seventeenth century.... Children's toys did not appear until 1600 and even then were not used beyond the age of three or four.... But by the late seventeenth century special artifacts for children were common. Also in the late seventeenth century we find the introduction of special childhood games ... *childhood did not apply to women.* The female child went from swaddling clothes right into adult female dress. She did not go to school, which, as we shall see, was the institution that structured childhood. At the age of nine or ten she acted, literally, like a 'little lady'; her activity did not differ from that of an adult woman. As soon as she reached puberty, as early as ten or twelve, she was married off to a much older male.[51]

A history of childhood then, is not regarded as a description of a succession of events, rather it is seen as providing the moral grounds of current speech about the child, and the family, and the unfinished business or unwritten story of the contemporary adult.

Second, the child can be approached comparatively, employing anthropological material. Here we might treat different child-rearing practices as aspects of culture. Mead's[52] work is instructive here in showing us how in different, yet contemporary, societies children assume far more autonomy and responsibility than is familiar within our own world.

> It may be said that where we are concerned with character formation – the process by which children discipline impulses and structure their expectations of the behavior of others – this cross-cultural approach is very valuable. It provides insights into such subjects as conscience formation, the relative importance of different sanctioning systems, sin, shame and pride, and guilt, and into the relationship between independence training and achievement motivation.[53]

Apart from adding to our understanding of the infinite variety of childhood(s), such an approach may also serve to deflate much of the ethnocentrism that is inherent in a Western sense of maturation. Boyden, using material from anthropology and development studies, makes the point that the exportation and globalization of a singular view of childhood from advanced Western capitalist societies can have a serious impact on the lives of children in developing countries:

> Despite extreme social and cultural diversity, there exists a core ideology in the South [developing countries], around which official versions of childhood pivot. This ideology dictates that children are demarcated from adults by a series of biological and psychological, as opposed to social, characteristics that are universally valid. It also dictates that childhood is accompanied by a set of rights that can be enshrined in international law.[54]

Finally, a phenomenological perspective could enable us to gain insight into an existential and generative sense of sociality that emerges from within the consciousness of the child. Merleau-Ponty,[55] for example, has demonstrated the acquisition of new linguistic forms by the child, due not so much to teaching as to personal, and intentional, affective experience. And Rafky, developing a phenomenology of the child, stated that:

> the life-world the newborn enters contains more than objects and social institutions. It is also charcterized by a complex of legitimations which explain and integrate the various action patterns of a group, a 'matrix of all socially objectivated and subjectively real meanings; the entire historic society and the entire biography of the individual are seen as events taking place within this universe' [Berger and Luckmann]. In short, the individual has acquired a set or mode for interpreting the world meaningfully; he perceives it in an ordered and subjectively understandable frame of reference.[56]

These three examples – the historical, the comparative and the phenomenological – are suggestions for alternative and instructive approaches to the study of childhood, all of which have been and continue to be explored within the area of 'childhood studies'. They do not in themselves constitute an exhaustive typology of programmes for research into childhood and they do not include an emergent concern for the 'perspective of the child'. This latter set of interests is not merely an extension of a concern within children's needs and rights, though it is in part, but beyond that it constitutes a serious attempt to speak the inarticulate and produce the child's world view. This certainly is a voice to be heard and one that is explored through innovative methodologies such as 'story telling'. We must beware, however, of any truth claims stemming from such work in excess of their accounts being more than an additional perspective. As sociologists are aware, we do not have to be Caesar in order to explain Caesar. Mayall made an important summation of such work when she stated that it is:

> concerned to study such topics as: to what extent child-hood belongs to children – or to adults; whether children's understanding of childhood can serve as a basis for reconstructing childhood; whether the development of a sociology of childhood is, can be and should be for children or for adults; what contributions can be made by adult observation and study of children to understanding childhood; what are the methodological and ethical issues intrinsic to collecting data from and with children and to providing accounts based on the data.[57]

Sociology is then beginning to find its way towards a sociology of childhood and it still has a degree of exciting exploratory work to do. A major contribution to consolidating such research was provided by James and Prout[58] in their groundbreaking work which attempted to establish a 'new paradigm' in the development of childhood sociology. I believe that it is worth quoting it here, in full:

> The key features of the paradigm:
> 1. Childhood is understood as a social construction. As such it provides an interpretive frame for contextualizing the early years of human life. Childhood, as distinct from biological immaturity, is neither a natural nor a universal feature of human groups but appears as a specific structural and cultural component of many societies.
> 2. Childhood is a variable of social analysis. It can never be entirely divorced from other variables such as class, gender or ethnicity. Comparative

and cross-cultural analysis reveals a variety of childhoods rather than a single or universal phenomenon.

3. Children's social relationships and cultures are worthy of study in their own right, independent of the perspective and concern of adults.

4. Children are and must be seen as active in the construction and determination of their own social lives, the lives of those around them and of the societies in which they live. Children are not just passive subjects of social structures and processes.

5. Ethnography is a particularly useful methodology for the study of childhood. It allows children a more direct voice and participation in the production of sociological data than is usually possible through experimental or survey styles of research.

6. Childhood is a phenomenon in relation to which the double hermeneutic of the social sciences is acutely present. That is to say, to proclaim a new paradigm of childhood sociology is also to engage in and respond to the process of reconstructing childhood.[59]

CONCLUSION

It is, perhaps, only through attempting to shift our concerns from the material child to the ideal, or to the 'vision' of the child, that sociology, and thus any sociology of the child, can prise itself free of a commitment to bolstering up the 'old order' in society (a major legacy of Comte's programme of positivist reconstruction) and begin to address the moral imperative of its manifesto, that is, a theorizing of the ever-emergent 'new order'. Indeed, within the extent and compass of a post-modern society such a shift is crucial for the survival of sociology itself,[60] it cannot remain wedded to old stories (or 'grand narratives'). Thus sociology's own continued development may find direction in an attention to the sociology of child development. In the next chapter we will look at the idea of visions of childhood in greater depth and attempt to relate such visions to their socio-historical contexts.

NOTES

[1] C. Jenks, *The Sociology of Childhood*, London: Batsford, 1982 (and Aldershot: Gregg Revivals, 1992); A. James and A. Prout, *Constructing and Reconstructing Childhood*, Basingstoke: Falmer, 1990; J. Qvortrup, *Childhood as a Social Phenomenon*, Vienna: The European Centre, 1993; W. Stainton-Rogers, *Child Abuse and Neglect*, Milton Keynes: Open University Press, 1991; C. Jenks, 'Social theorizing and the child: constraints and possibilities' in S. Doxiadis (ed.), *Early Influences Shaping the Individual*, NATO Advanced Study Workshop, London: Plenum Press, 1989.

[2] A. Schutz, *Collected Papers, Vol. 1*, The Hague: Martinus Nijhoff, 1964; H. Garfinkel, *Studies in Ethnomethodology*, Englewood Cliffs: Prentice-Hall, 1967.

[3] H. Hendrick, 'Constructions and reconstructions of British childhood: an interpretive survey, 1800 to the present' in A. James and A. Prout (eds), *Constructing and Reconstructing Childhood*, Basingstoke: Falmer, 1990.

[4] Ibid., p. 35.

[5] See R. Fletcher (ed.), *Auguste Comte and the Making of Sociology*, London: Nelson, 1972.

[6] K. Thompson, *August Comte: The Foundation of Sociology*, London: Nelson, 1976, p. 13.

[7] E. Durkheim, *The Rules of Sociological Method*, New York: Free Press, 1938.

[8] P. Hirst, *Durkheim, Bernard and Epistemology*, London: Routledge & Kegan Paul, 1975.

[9] E. Durkheim, *The Rules of the Sociological Method* (trans. W. Halls), London: Macmillan, 1982, p. 35.

[10] T. Parsons, *The Structure of Social Action*, New York: Free Press, 1968.

[11] A. Cicourel, *Method and Measurement in Sociology*, New York: Free Press, 1964; A. Dawe, 'Two sociologies' in *British Journal of Sociology*, 1970; D. Wrong, 'The oversocialized conception of man in modern sociology' in *American Sociological Review*, XXVI, April 1961; M. Hollis, *Models of Man*, Cambridge: Cambridge University Press, 1977.

[12] J. O'Neill, *The Missing Child in Liberal Theory*, Toronto: University of Toronto Press, 1994, p. 54.

[13] A. Giddens, *Modernity and Self-identity*, Cambridge, Polity

Press, 1991; U. Beck, *Risk Society: Towards a New Modernity*, London: Sage, 1992.

[14] R. MacKay, 'Conceptions of children and models of socialization' in H. P. Dreitzel (ed.), *Recent Sociology No. 5 – Childhood and Socialization*, New York: Macmillan, 1973, p. 27.

[15] J. Piaget, *The Language and Thought of the Child*, London: Routledge & Kegan Paul, 1977.

[16] G. Frank, *The Sociology of Development and the Undevelopment of Sociology*, London: Pluto Press, 1971.

[17] C. Jenks, *Rationality, Education and the Social Organization of Knowledge*, London: Routledge & Kegan Paul, 1977; L. Wittgenstein; *Philosophical Investigations*, Oxford: Blackwell, 1967.

[18] A. James and A. Prout (eds), op. cit., p. 216.

[19] Such writers as Lombrosso, Jensen and Eysenck, and Kraepelin.

[20] C. Hendricks and J. Hendricks, 'Historical developments of the multiplicity of time and implications for the analysis of ageing' in *The Human Context*, vol. VII, The Hague: Martinus Nijhoff, 1975.

[21] E. Durkheim, *The Elementary Forms of the Religious Life*, London: Allen & Unwin, 1968, p. 214.

[22] J. Goldstein, A. Freud and A. J. Solnit, *Beyond the Best Interest of the Child*, New York: Free Press, 1973, p. 40.

[23] Warnock Committee, *Special Educational Needs*, London: HMSO/DES, 1978.

[24] L. DeMause, *The History of Childhood*, London: Souvenir, 1976; P. Coveney, *The Image of Childhood*, Harmondsworth: Penguin, 1967; J. Donzelot, *The Policing of Families*, London: Hutchinson, 1980.

[25] M. Merleau-Ponty, *The Primacy of Perception*, Paris: Gallimard, 1967; J. O'Neill, 'Embodiment and child development: a phenomenological approach' in H. Dreitzel (ed.), *Recent Sociology No. 5*, London: Macmillan, 1973.

[26] M. Hambrook, *Accounts of the Child–Adult Relationship in Sociology: With Special Reference to the Work of Piaget, Parsons and Freud*, unpublished M.Phil. thesis, University of London, 1987.

[27] A.-M. Ambert, 'An international perspective on parenting: social change and social constructs' in *Journal of Marriage and the Family*, 56, August 1994, p. 530.

[28] C. Jenks, 'Child abuse in the postmodern context: an issue

of social identity' in *Childhood*, vol. 3, 1994; H. Hendrick, 'Constructions and reconstructions of British childhood: an interpretive survey, 1800 to the present' in A. James and A. Prout (eds), op. cit.; W. Kessen, 'The child and other cultural inventions' in F. Kessel and A. Siegal (eds), *The Child and Other Cultural Inventions*, New York: Praeger, 1983.

[29] T. Parsons, *The Social System*, New York: Free Press, 1964; A. Schutz, *Collected Papers Vol. 1*, The Hague: Martinus Nijhoff, 1964.

[30] I. Illich, *Deschooling Society*, London: Calder & Boyers, 1971; N. Postman and C. Weingarten, *Teaching as a Subversive Activity*, Harmondsworth: Penguin, 1971; J. Holt, *Escape from Childhood*, Harmondsworth: Penguin, 1971.

[31] E. Durkheim, *The Division of Labour in Society*, New York: Free Press, 1933.

[32] C. Gilligan, J. Wood and J. McLean Taylor, *Mapping the Moral Domain: A Contribution of Women's Thinking to Psychological Theory and Education*, Cambridge, MA: Harvard University Press, 1988, p. 5.

[33] R. Williams, *Culture and Society 1780–1950*, London: Chatto & Windus, 1958.

[34] A.-M. Ambert, op. cit., p. 530.

[35] A. Gramsci, *The Modern Prince and Other Writings*, New York: International Publishers, 1970.

[36] P. Bourdieu, *Outline of a Theory of Practice*, Cambridge: Cambridge University Press, 1977.

[37] L. Althusser, *Lenin and Philosophy and Other Essays*, London: New Left Books, 1971.

[38] Ibid., p. 147.

[39] H. Marcuse, 'Repressive tolerance' in R. Wolff, C. Barrington Moore and H. Marcuse (eds), *A Critique of Tolerance*, Boston: Beacon, 1965.

[40] H. Marcuse, *One Dimensional Man*, London: Abacus, 1972, p. 16.

[41] Ibid., p. 195.

[42] P. Bourdieu and J. Passeron, *Reproduction in Education, Society and Culture*, London: Sage, 1977.

[43] P. Bourdieu, 'Systems of education and systems of thought' in *International Social Science Journal*, vol. XIX, 1967, pp. 192–193.

[44] Ibid., p. 195.

[45] M. Foucault, *Discipline and Punish*, London: Allen Lane, 1977.
[46] B. Bernstein, *Class, Codes and Control*, vols 1, 2 and 3, London: Routledge & Kegan Paul, 1971–3.
[47] A. Halsey, J. Floud and C. Anderson (eds), *Education, Economy and Society*, Glencoe, IL: Free Press, 1961; O. Banks, *The Sociology of Education*, London: Batsford, 1968.
[48] P. Willis, *Learning to Labour*, London: Gower, 1977.
[49] Ibid., p. 1.
[50] P. Ariès, *Centuries of Childhood*, London: Cape, 1973.
[51] S. Firestone, *The Dialectics of Sex*, London: Paladin, 1972, pp. 43–44.
[52] M. Mead, *Growing up in New Guinea*, Harmondsworth: Penguin, 1954.
[53] M. Mead, 'Early childhood experience and later education in complex cultures' in M. Wax *et al.* (eds), *Anthropological Perspectives on Education*, New York: Basic Books, 1971, p. 219.
[54] J. Boyden, 'Childhood and the policy makers: a comparative perspective on the globalization of childhood' in A. James and A. Prout (eds), op. cit., p. 184.
[55] M. Merleau-Ponty, *The Primacy of Perception*, Paris: Gallimard, 1967.
[56] D. Rafky, 'Phenomenology and socialization: some comments on the assumptions underlying socialization theories' in H. P. Dreitzel (ed.), op. cit., 1973, p. 43.
[57] B. Mayall (ed.), *Children's Childhoods: Observed and Experienced*, London: Falmer, 1994, p. 1.
[58] A. James and A. Prout, op. cit., 1990.
[59] Ibid., pp. 8–9.
[60] J.-F. Lyotard, *The Postmodern Condition: A Report on Knowledge*, Manchester: Manchester University Press, 1984.

3

The birth of childhood

Children . . . have no use for psychology. They detest sociology. They still believe in God, the family, angels, devils, witches, goblins, logic, clarity, punctuation and other such obsolete stuff. . . . When a book is boring, they yawn openly. They don't expect their writer to redeem humanity, but leave to adults such childish illusions.[1]

Over the last two decades, and with an accelerative intensity, sociology has, in the manner of Lévi-Strauss's primitive cosmologist, sought to transform the natural into the cultural. Its practice has been dedicated to the desecration of images and realities previously enshrined in the sacred realm of utter naturalness. In modern parlance it has therefore rendered the mundane and taken-for-granted problematic. Now in one sense this is nothing new, it always has been sociology's project. Durkheim was adamant that the social should always be explained in terms of the social and each of his theses, from suicide to religion, is polemical in its sustained assaults on all other attempts to explain and thus appropriate his chosen phenomenon through extra-social forms of discourse. Durkheim would also have approved of what might

appear as a methodological appropriation that engulfs all
phenomena within its territory and leaves no natural state of
affairs free to explain itself, without social structures. In this one
sense, such modern initiatives complete Comte's law of three
stages, that we considered in the last chapter, by ensuring that
sociology should transcend all other forms of explanation; but
this is only one sense, albeit an important one.

To a greater extent these modern sociological developments
have been motivated by a different politic. The contemporary
debunkings of the kind of reasoning which runs 'it's only human
nature . . .', have all been part of an emergent attitude towards
the revelation of more and yet more covert forms of social stratification within an advanced, capitalist, division of labour. This
attitude is driven by a compulsive urge to re-democratize the
grounds of all existing social relations.

Sociology was grounded on the canon that the natural divisions between people (though primarily men) should be properly
understood as issues of social class, and although this is an auspice
for theorizing most closely identified with Marx, it is also clearly
central to the ideas of Durkheim and Weber. The discourse of
stratification thus, for a considerable period, became enshrined
in the language of social class. Modern sociology has opened up
the parameters of such discourse and taken it beyond social class,
quite often at the expense of social class. Modern sociology has
en-culturated, primarily, the natural realms of sex, which we now
know to be an issue of gender, and race, which is thus to be understood in terms of ethnicity; more recent frontiers are those of age,
sexuality and disability. Noting this tendency in the social sciences,
and its sequential delays and subsequent injustices, Elshtain has
stated:

> For many reasons . . . children have been the companions
> of women in the closet of political science. A few short
> years ago women began to set up such a clamour that a
> few were released. . . . Children remain, with few excep-
> tions, both silent and invisible – relegated to a conceptual
> space (which is presumed to reflect social reality) that has
> been declared apolitical. The political study of childhood
> remains in its infancy.[2]

During the 1970s in the UK a great deal of the innovations
in sociological theory emerged through a then dynamic area of
study – the sociology of education. This branch of sociology had

been ignited during the 1960s in the work of the statistical Fabian demographers such as Glass, Halsey and Floud but then exploded into a variety of new perspectives. Neo-marxisms vied with symbolic interaction, ethnomethodology and phenomenology but all of these interpretive paradigms coalesced around the single view that education, in form and content, was a social construct. This generation of scholars who were party to and instrumental in the 1968 Revolution still believed that education was a vehicle for social change; a belief deriving, in many cases, from personal experience rather than from structural evidence. Their research set about revealing the constraints placed upon this process by patterns inherent in forms of the curriculum – the single most significant social construct of them all. In my own work of that period I gradually confronted the irony of a phenomenologically constituted view of the curriculum populated by non-intentional actors. Who were these silent recipients of the curriculum complex, were they essentially different to the social roles, peer group orientations, deferred gratifications, contest mobilities and general socialization-theory fodder that I had so vehemently rejected in the past? I had a need for real, active, children; but not actually, this was a naturalistic reduction. I had a need to articulate childhood, the state of being within culture, the way that different societies and different epochs represented this ontology, acted in relation to such imagery and thus variously enabled the emergent qualities of its newness. To this end I assembled and integrated a series of readings that seemed to express this important theme – this I published in 1982 as *The Sociology of Childhood*.[3] I had de-naturalized the child, I had discovered the sociology of childhood; well, I had given it a name and its development would prove to be far more influential and significant than its christening.

I came to see that our collective images of childhood and our subsequent relations with children could be regarded as indices of the contemporary state of the social structure – this formulation was familiar but not one I had arrived at with the assistance of Husserl, Heidegger or Merleau-Ponty, the writers currently informing my thinking. No, the idea derived from a very different source, it was Emile Durkheim speaking, 'the' father of our discipline and the figure who was routinely derided by undergraduates of that period as a 'functionalist', 'positivist' and 'empiricist' – all of the things known to be bad and provide good reason for never reading the original works. I had arrived at the interminable problem of attempting to explain the relationship between the symbolic order and the social structure; this was the problem most clearly established by Durkheim in *The Division of Labour* and refined, though not exhausted, in *Primitive Classification* and *The Elementary Forms of the Religious Life*. This was the problem adopted by Durkheim's living heir, Basil Bernstein, who would go on to write Durkheim's previously nascent theory of socialization and develop his implicit theory of social consciousness. Bernstein's work, in generating an excitingly original sociolinguistic framework for the explanation of cultural reproduction and through his constructive thesis on the social organization of the educational dimensions of curriculum, pedagogy and evaluation was, in many senses, to complete Durkheim's project. Bernstein's method proceeds from appearance and works towards actual form through a peeling away of layers. As Douglas has explained:

> Whatever he does, whether analyzing how a mother controls her child, how a teacher teaches, how a patient confronts a psychoanalyst, how the curriculum is worked out in a school or college, he looks at four elements in the social process. First, the system of control; second, the boundaries it sets up; third, the justification or ideology which sanctifies the boundaries; and fourth, the power itself which is hidden by the rest. The analysis always ends by revealing the distribution of power. This is the trick of demystification.[4]

Bernstein, it appeared to me, had been talking about children all the time. Not real, embodied children as the clients of the educational system but metaphors for the different forms of consciousness within different realizations of solidarity. Mediated through the 'codes' Bernstein had produced two models of fresh, not natural but enculturated, childhood consciousness – they were both the intentional and structural constituents of the social bond. The history, imagery and contextualization of these models became my substantive interest, as I shall show in this chapter.

THE EMERGENCE OF CHILDHOOD

Although it is clearly the case that children are omnipresent in human society both across space and through time, it is nevertheless true to say that childhood is a relatively recent phenomenon in the social sciences. As Mead and Wolfenstein told us: 'Although each historical period of which we have any record has had its own version of childhood ... childhood was still something that one took for granted, a figure of speech, a mythological subject rather than a subject of articulate scrutiny.'[5] It would appear that the idea of childhood only emerged at a comparatively late stage in the historical process. This is an idea propounded by many theorists including Hoyles who plainly stated: 'Both childhood and our present day nuclear family are comparatively recent inventions.'[6]

Similarly Zelizer,[7] addressing the relatively recent epoch straddling the turn of the nineteenth and twentieth centuries in the USA, invokes the term 'sacralization' to discuss the remarkable transformations that seem to have occurred in the economic and affective value of children during that period. By investigating the changing attitudes, in both families and the public at large, towards child labour, child mortality, child care, adoption and abandonment she argues that children shifted from having low economic worth to immeasurable, or 'priceless', emotional value.

This contemporary topicality is itself an instance of the thesis that this chapter will seek to unravel. That a state of being, such as childhood, should be formulated through the 'analytic gaze' within a particular epoch must tell us as much about the condition of our society as it does about our children.

Today children are everywhere thought of as normal. As such common sense is redolent with images and understandings that contrive to produce the child not just as normal but also as utterly natural. Yet as Hoyles asserted: 'Childhood is a social convention and not just a natural state.'[8]

Seemingly, the absolute necessity of children as real presences throughout history, as opposed to the temporary and fragile character of other phenomena such as capitalism, HIV and the European Community – however serious their impact on human beings – has rendered childhood completely mundane; we simply take it for granted.[9] Unlike the poor, in reality it is children who are always with us. As an event childhood is not even different enough to specify a mode of experience that is peculiar to certain groups of people; it is what everyone does or has done at a stage in their lives. Beyond this childhood is a transitory phenomenon, we 'grow out of it', it is routinely disregarded on our way to achieving our proper destiny; adult rational life. This normative assumption is reflected in our chastisement of people for 'acting childishly'. Being grown-up must surely be the purpose of being!

Now such an elaboration of what everyone knows about childhood is not particularly informative. My intention in rehearsing such ideas is to indicate the embeddedness of our 'knowing' about children in conceptions of the 'normal' and the 'natural'. We must shift our perspective to another site. Childhood is not a brief physical inhabitation of a Lilliputian world owned and ruled by others, childhood is rather a historical and cultural experience and its meaning, its interpretations and its interests reside within such contexts. These contexts, these social structures, become our topic. It is here where normative expectations arise and it is to an analysis of such structures that we shall proceed. As Cunningham stated in his masterly endeavour to transform the adult 'story' of childhood into an embodied, material history of childhood:

> The construction of childhood is of course a continuing process: 'childhood' is never fixed and constant. But between the late seventeenth and mid-twentieth centuries there occurred a major and irreversible change in the representations of childhood, to the point where all children throughout the world were thought to be entitled to certain common elements and rights of childhood. Often they did not receive them, but one should not doubt the importance of the claims made on behalf of children. Until now ... the process by which those claims were made has been known to us in the form of a story; I hope ... to begin to see it as a history.[10]

What I cannot aspire to, in a work of this scale, is a chronology of the changing images of the child and patterns of child care through history; this is a majoi task and has been attempted in a number of sources, despite the methodological problems noted by Stainton-Rogers: 'Of all social groups which formed societies of the past, children, seldom seen and rarely heard in the document, remain for historians the most elusive, the most obscure.'[11]

We should also note the instructive and cautionary note put forward by Steedman in precisely this context:

> Historiographical difficulties lie in the way of discussing the history of childhood ... it is worth discussing them

at this juncture. To start with, it has often been noted that the history of childhood is intensely teleological, much of it presented to illustrate a progress made by a society towards an enlightened present. In this version of history, a horrific past – child labour, or child exploitation, or child abuse – is overtly presented as a counterpoint to current circumstances. . . . But this teleology is in fact extremely difficult to abandon, for we live and write history by a central tenet of nineteenth-century reforming liberalism, which tells us that one measure of a society's civilisation and progress is to be found in its treatment of disadvantaged and dispossessed groups: women, slaves and children.[12]

And this, in part, takes us back to reflect upon the campaigning politics of much contemporary sociology with which this chapter began.

CENTURIES OF CHILDHOOD

In an effort to establish a diachronicity of childhood cultural experience, an exercise positively formative in the establishment of socio-childhood studies, a number of highly influential post-Enlightenment histories have emerged witnessing the chronology of the changing images of the child and patterns of child care. The leading figure in producing such a history, or perhaps archaeology, of images of childhood is Ariès,[13] whom I have previously referred to; his ideas provide a focus for much subsequent theorizing about the child. We note that Ariès argues from material drawn mostly from French culture, but it is conventionally supposed that his thesis is generalizable in relation to the development of the rest of the modern Western world, and as such it is wholly disruptive of common-sense views of the child.

Primarily Ariès is informing us that there was a time before which children were invisible. Up to and including the Middle Ages it would seem that there was no collective perception of children as being essentially different to anyone else. People populated the world but their status was not established in terms of their age nor their physical maturity. This is very challenging, and, at first hearing, it is a difficult proposition to accept as we have already conceded the proposition that children are a fact and the truism that they have always been with us. However, what Ariès is illuminating is that the manner of their recognition by adults, their re-presentations, and thus the forms of their relationships with adults, has altered through the passage of time. This idea becomes more easy to assimilate when we reflect on the more recent invention of the 'youth', 'adolescent' or 'teenager' in Western society over, perhaps, the period since the Second World War. Here we have a quite clearly distinguishable group of people within our society (albeit only within the Western world) who occupy a now firmly established twilight zone of the quasi-child or crypto-adult.

To return from this example to Ariès, he is arguing that children have not always existed in the way that we now know them, they have not always been the same thing. In the Middle Ages, he states, there was no concept of childhood and it is from this absence that our current view of the child has evolved. Ancient society, we are told, may well have understood the difference of childhood and grasped the necessity of children's development, whereas medieval civilization seems to have either abandoned or mislaid such a recognition to await its rediscovery in modernity.

> Medieval civilization had forgotten the *paideia* of the ancients and knew nothing as yet of modern education. That is the main point: it had no idea of education. Nowadays our society depends, and knows that it depends, on the success of its education system. It has a system of education, a concept of education, an awareness of its importance. New sciences such as psycho-analysis, pediatrics and psychology devote themselves to the problems of childhood, and their findings are transmitted to parents by way of a mass of popular literature. Our world is obsessed by the physical, moral and sexual problems of children.[14]

The reason for this loss, or cultural amnesia, in medieval times is unexplained but the evidence of its impact Ariès derives from a study of painting and iconography: 'Medieval art until about the twelfth century did not know childhood or did not attempt to portray it. It is hard to believe that this neglect was due to incompetence or incapacity; it seems more probable that there was no place for childhood in the medieval world.'[15]

It is, in fact, the case that the figurative painting of the Middle Ages is notable for its dearth of depictions of children. They were apparently considered of such little importance that they did not warrant representation in a unique and particular form. Where such images do occur, as by necessity in the motif of the Madonna and child, the baby Jesus appears uniformly, from example to example, as a small shrunken man, a wizened homonculus without the rounded appeal and vulnerability of the latter-day infant. This then is our baseline, a world seemingly without the visual recognition of children. We have to imagine a world in which people are differentiated only by their place in the division of labour, part of which, presumably, is the pre-labouring stage of being weaned.

> In medieval society the idea of childhood did not exist; this is not to suggest that children were neglected, forsaken or despised. The idea of childhood is not to be confused with affection for children: it corresponds to an awareness of the particular nature of childhood, that particular nature which distinguishes the child from the adult, even the young adult. In medieval society this awareness was lacking. That is why, as soon as the child could live without the constant solicitude of his mother, his nanny or his cradle-rocker, he belonged to adult society.[16] – a worker, a provider - able to have a r/ship to be married - + able to have a child of their own

This is an important point later supported by Illich who stated that: 'Childhood as distinct from infancy, adolescence or youth was unknown to most historical periods ... the peasant's child and the nobleman's child all dressed and played as their Fathers.'[17] Ariès now takes us on a journey to the present.

Following in the wake of the Middle Ages, children, in history, emerged initially as playthings. They were not separate, segregated or insulated from the adult world but provided it with delight or entertainment. Thus, according to Ariès, although through the sixteenth and into the seventeenth century people took pleasure in pampering or 'coddling' their children, they were only gradually beginning to realize their presence as a distinct way of being in the world. It would, of course, be a mistake to imagine that this adult awakening was in any sense a universal response to the emergent condition of infancy. Only particular privileged groups or classes within society could afford the luxury of childhood with its demands on material provision, time and emotion and its attendant paraphernalia of toys and special clothing. For most people children remained an inevitability, realizable as a potential source of contribution to the economy of the family. Large families were both an investment in human capital and a hedge against infant mortality. This social stratification in the recognition and understanding of childhood stretches right up until the twentieth century, as Steedman has informed us in relation to the British example:

> In the late nineteenth century, and in the years up to the First World War, childhood was reconceptualised in British society – that is to say, children became the subjects of legislative attention and formed the basis of various accounts of social development as they had not done before. In a range of social and aesthetic criticism a historical process was often described whereby attention had first of all been directed at the children of the wealthier classes. Later in the century, it was then argued, the children of the poor became the beneficiaries of the increased understanding of the nature of childhood.[18]

Ariès locates the genesis of the modern conception of the child in the eighteenth century and this is a view that is shared throughout the body of the literature that I am referring to as post-Enlightenment histories. Robertson, for example, stated that:

> If the philosophy of the Enlightenment brought to eighteenth century Europe a new confidence in the possibility of human happiness, special credit must go to Rousseau for calling attention to the needs of children. For the first time in history, he made a large group of people believe that childhood was worth the attention of intelligent adults, encouraging an interest in the process of growing up rather than just the product. Education of children was part of the interest in progress which was so predominant in the intellectual trends of the time.[19]

Children, through this period of the Enlightenment, had, it would seem, escaped into difference. We witness the arrival of a new category of being, one that is fresh and frail and consequently a target for correction and training by the growing standards of rationality that came to pervade the time. Once a concern with the child's physical health and well-being had been institutionalized, along with an attention to their moral welfare, then our model for modernity is almost complete. The child has moved through time from obscurity to the centre stage. The child is forever assured the spotlight of public policy and attention and also a primary place in the family. Indeed one might argue that the family has come to be defined in terms of the child's presence. In a more poetic vein Cunningham has added that:

> This new privileged status of childhood entailed more than a perceived separateness of child and adult. From the time of the Romantic poets onwards it is not uncommon to see childhood as a repository of inheritances and attributes which were often lost or blunted in adulthood. The more adults and adult society seemed bleak, urbanized and alienated, the more childhood came to be seen as properly a garden, enclosing within the safety of its walls a way of life which was in touch with nature and which preserved the rude virtues of earlier periods of the history of mankind. Some, like Dickens, hoped that this child life and these child virtues could be kept alive in the adult. Others, later, for example J. M. Barrie, experienced a sense of profound loss; he could recapture his own childhood only by inflicting an imagined version of it on other children. In both cases the polarity of child and adult was implicit if regretted; the child was 'the other' for which one yearned.[20]

We should note that the thesis provided by Ariès is both persuasive and formative; however, alternative and critical accounts have been presented, and well gathered, by Pollock[21] who was driven at one point in her thesis to state, rather pessimistically, that: 'Some writers feel that the sources which are available for the history of childhood are so problematic that the subject cannot be studied.'[22] Fortunately historians of the child have not desisted and the critiques of Ariès rarely succeed in achieving more than a modification of his central ideas. For Ariès the history of childhood is a transition from darkness into light and he sets out not just a pattern for future analysis but also an optimism and a justification of modern-day child-rearing that we might properly treat with caution.

DeMause,[23] in similar vein, is most expressive of the dark side and thus over-enthusiastic concerning the illuminating potential of today's parenting. His haunting and wildly exaggerated vision of the history of childhood is that of a nightmare:

> The history of childhood is a nightmare from which we

have only recently begun to awake. . . . The further back in history one goes, the lower the level of child care, and the more likely children are to be killed, abandoned, beaten, terrorised and sexually abused.[24]

DeMause proposes what he calls a 'psychogenic theory of history' which revolves around the notion that history consists in the evolution of the human personality brought about through successive and positive developments in the relationship between parents and children. The stages in this process that he puts forward begin with the routine infanticide of antiquity and conclude with the partially realized 'Helping Mode' of the late twentieth century; the latter being a kind of systematic, and empathetic, facilitation of the child's unique intent through maturation. Although DeMause is not so mechanistic as to suggest that this historical process has been a strictly linear one its paradigmatic or serpentine development retains, however, the unequivocal commitment to the view that now, for children, there is 'heaven' and once there was 'hell'; a truly Enlightenment conflation between culture and civilization.

The last in my inventory of childhood evolutionists, though there are many more, is Shorter.[25] His work is unctuously congratulatory of the humane achievements in child-rearing that have come to be crystallized in the form of today's nuclear family. Our changing attitudes have apparently transformed children from the status of object, worthy only of disregard, into the status of subject, and subject of our central attention and self-sacrifice. 'Good mothering', we are informed, 'is an invention of modernisation.'[26]

The point, I trust, is clear. This strand of progressive moral paediatrics provides a convincing account of the child, through history, and has metamorphosed into an ontology. The child has become a subject in its own right, a source of identity and more than this, a promise of the future good. The child has come to symbolize all that is decent and caring about a society, it is the very index of a civilization – witness the outrage and general moral disapproval at the revelations concerning Romanian orphanages, an obvious signifier of the corruption of Communist social structures!

CHILDHOOD AND SOCIAL CONTROL

In the analysis that follows I concur with the thesis concerning the emergence of childhood images so far stated, but only so far. It is a theory not without tropes and a process laden with ironies. The modern image of the child is one that is clear, visible and in need of containment. The historical liberation of the child from adulthood has led, in turn, to the necessity of its constraint by collective practices. The obvious high profile of children in our contemporary patterns of relationship has rendered them subject to new forms of control. As Rose has informed us in his work on the growth of control over personhood in the twentieth century:

> Childhood is the most intensively governed sector of personal existence. In different ways, at different times, and by many different routes varying from one section of society to another, the health, welfare, and rearing of children have been linked in thought and practice to the destiny of the nation and the responsibilities of the state. The modern child has become the focus of innumerable projects that purport to safeguard it from physical, sexual, and moral danger, to ensure its 'normal' development, to actively promote certain capacities of attributes such as intelligence, educability and emotional stability.[27]

Similarly, just as the delineation of the child's particularity has given rise to specially fashioned forms of control so also has the diminution of public ignorance and disdain towards the child privatized new and intrusive forms of violence extending from neurotic families to parental sexual abuse.

What I will produce is a framework for an analysis of the shifting patterns of normality that have been applied to the child through the massive turbulence, upheaval and transformations that occurred in Europe with the advent of the Modern Age. This is the period that brought sociology itself into being and was marked by the acceleration of a number of significant structural processes such as the division of labour, industrialization, urbanization, the market economy and the secularization of belief systems away from the consensual obedience to the deity towards an allegiance to the necessities of science, technology and progress through growth.

The analysis will depend on the assumption that its subject – in this case childhood – emerges from a particular structuring of social relationships and that its various meanings derive from the forms of discourse that accompany those relationships. Childhood appears in different forms in different cultures in relation to structural variables such as rates of mortality and life expectancy, organizations of family life and structure, kinship patterns, and different ideologies of care and philosophies of need and dependency. A discourse providing for childhood in modern Western society might be that of a paediatrician, a parent, a teacher or an educational psychologist; or equally well those of a television producer and an advertising executive.[28]

These different forms of discourse clearly do not have an equivalence. They move in and out of focus according to the different aspects of the subject that are being considered. Sometimes this occurs in parallel but sometimes in competition, and often such discourses are arranged hierarchically, for example, in specific the child-discourse of social workers or juvenile magistrates have a power and efficacy in excess of those of the sibling or parent. But all such discourses contribute to and, in turn, derive from the dominant cultural image of the 'normal' child. This, of necessity, implies that the child is part of a social structure and thus functional within a network of relations, a matrix of partial interests and a complex of forms of professional knowledge that are beyond the physical experience of being a child.

To draw once again on the work of Hillman, writing in relation to analytical psychology, he states that: 'Whatever we say about children and childhood is not altogether really about children and childhood.'[29] He is, in the original context, referring to childhood as a causal repository for the explanation of self and the progress of the psyche, but he may equally be read as suggesting that theories of the child are always pointers towards the social construction of reality. Just as I have argued that the child is neither simply 'natural' nor merely 'normal', we may claim to have established, in addition, that the child is not neutral but rather always moral and political. Thus the way that we treat our children is indicative of the state of our social structure, a measure of the achievement of our civilization or even an index of the degree to which humanism has outstripped the economic motive in everyday life. Similarly, the way that we control our children reflects, perhaps as a continuous microcosm, the strategies through which we exercise power and constraint in the wider society. For Durkheim,[30] quite clearly, the purpose of pedagogic theory and practice, as the formal mode of socialization, is to ensure the quality and achievement of a society through the necessary process of cultural reproduction. For others, like Bourdieu and Passeron,[31] socialization is the mechanism through which we continue to confer power and privilege through the investment of 'cultural capital' by virtue of the unnecessary process of social stratification.

Throughout the historical and cross-cultural literature on childhood what seems to emerge are two dominant ways of talking and thinking about children (which we might refer to as 'codes'); two traditions of conceptualizing the child that although, at different times, practically supported and reinforced by various religious beliefs, political ideologies and scientific doctrines, are too old and pervasive to be explained in terms of such cultural regimes. For this reason I shall formulate them as images arising from mythology – myths being the devices that people have always employed to account for anomalies or the seemingly inexplicable in their cosmologies. Boas[32] made the original link between childhood and mythology, an idea that has later been amplified by Rose with reference to children's literature:

> As a myth of our culture, *Peter Pan* shares with other myths a place which seems to transcend the local and historical conditions out of which it first emerged. As a myth of childhood, it adds to that transcendence the particular force of innocence. Myth and childhood belong together, in that myth is so often identified with what is primitive, even *infantile*, or is seen as a form of expression which goes back to the origins of culture and speech.[33]

The two mythological images invoked here I shall refer to as the Dionysian and the Apollonian views of childhood. To add to the complexity of these configurations I shall suggest that although they are competitive to the point of absolute incompatibility, within cultures they are used to understand childhood primarily through history but also synchronically, that is in parallel at the same time.

THE DIONYSIAN CHILD

What I am calling the Dionysian image rests on the assumption of an initial evil or corruption within the child – Dionysus being the prince of wine, revelry and nature. A major buttress to such imagery can be found in the doctrine of Adamic original sin.

Children, it is supposed, enter the world as a wilful material force, they are impish and harbour a potential evil. This primal force will be mobilized if, in any part, the adult world should allow them to stray away from the appropriate path that the blueprint of human culture has provided for them. Such children must not fall into bad company, establish bad habits, or develop idle hands – all of these contexts will enable outlets for the demonic force within, which is, of course, potentially destructive not just of the child but also of the adult collectivity. The child is Dionysian in as much as it loves pleasure, it celebrates self-gratification and it is wholly demanding in relation to any object, or indeed subject, that prevents its satiation. The intrusive noise that is childhood is expressive of a single-minded solipsistic array of demands in relation to which all other interests become peripheral and all other presences become satellites to enabling this goal.

Christianity has provided a significant contribution to this way of regarding the child even though, as Shipman[34] has pointed out, the fall in infant mortality through modernity has reduced our urgency and anxiety about their state of grace at an early age. Ariès directs us to the sixteenth-century view of the child as weak, which was accompanied by the practice of 'coddling'; but this was not a weakness in the sense of vulnerability so much as a weakness in the form of susceptibility to corruption and being 'easily led'. Parenting consequently consisted of distant and strict moral guidance, through physical direction. Stemming from this period, in the tradition of this image, a severe view of the child is sustained, one that saw socialization as almost a battle but certainly a form of combat where the headstrong and stubborn subject had to be 'broken', but all for their own good. This harsh campaign of child-rearing persisted through the Puritanism of the seventeenth century, with rods not being spared in order to spoil children, and even on into the nineteenth century with an evangelical zeal that sought out and waged war on the depravity of drunkenness, idleness or childhood wherever it was found. Dickens is a great source of such tales of our institutionalized violence towards the young, and Coveney[35] provides a fine collection and analysis of this image of the child, embattled by materialism, throughout literature:

> In this context of isolation, alienation, doubt and intellec-
> tual conflict, it is not difficult to see the attraction of the

child as a literary theme. The child could serve as a symbol of the artist's dissatisfaction with a society which was in process of such harsh development about him. In a world given increasingly to utilitarian values and the Machine, the child could become the symbol of Imagination and Sensibility, a symbol of Nature set against the forces abroad in society actively de-naturing humanity. Through the child the artist could express his awareness of the conflict between human Innocence and the cumulative pressures of social Experience. If the central problem of the artist was in fact one of adjustment, one can see the possibilities for identification between the artist and the consciousness of the child whose difficulty and chief source of pain often lie in adjustment and accommodation to environment. In childhood lay the perfect image of insecurity and isolation, of fear and bewilderment, of vulnerability and potential violation.[36]

In practical terms the Dionysian child was being deafened, blinded and exploited through factory labour, and still being sent up chimneys with brushes as late as 1850 – in Britain alone!

It would be convenient to regard what I am calling the Dionysian child as an image of a former time, a set of ideas belonging to a simpler, more primitive people than our own, and to some degree this is so. However, we must not disregard the systematic secular exploration of the soul that has been practised and recommended by psychoanalysis throughout the last century. It was Freud who most recently and forcefully formulated this image of the child through his concept of the id and in relation to his theory of infantile sexuality. Of the triumvirate that comprise the self for Freud, the super-ego is the possession of the collectivity, the e.g.o the realm of the adult and the id (together with its immature adult counterpart 'neurosis') the special province of the child. The id, as we know, is that libidinal repository of insatiable desire. It is the dark driving force which acts as the source of all creativity yet which is required to be quelled or 'repressed' such that people can live in relation to one another and have some regard for the mutual incompatibility of their systems of desire. The social bond resides in this repression; the story of and its implications for child-rearing are familiar, if more subtle. And Freud's narrative has had a global impact on the understanding of childhood, as Millar has pointed out: 'We owe the fundamental recognition of the significance of early childhood for all later life to Sigmund Freud – a discovery that is probably valid for every society in every period of history.'[37]

THE APOLLONIAN CHILD

What now of the Apollonian child, the heir to the sunshine and light, the espouser of poetry and beauty? This does appear to be, much more, the modern, Western, but only 'public', way of regarding the child. Such infants are angelic, innocent and untainted by the world which they have recently entered. They have a natural goodness and a clarity of vision that we might 'idolize' or even 'worship' as the source of all that is best in human nature (note the character of these two metaphors 'idolize' and 'worship', so often used to denote the love relation between parent and child). Such children play and chuckle, smile and laugh, both spontaneously but also with our sustained encouragement. We cannot abide their tears and tantrums, we want only the illumination from their halo. This is humankind before either Eve or the apple. It is within this model that we honour and celebrate the child and dedicate ourselves to reveal its newness and uniqueness. Gone are the strictures of uniformity, here, with romantic vision, we explore the particularity of the person. Such thinking has been instructive of all child-centred learning and special-needs education from Montessori, the Plowden Report, A. S. Neill and the Warnock Report, and indeed much of primary teaching in the last three decades. This Apollonian image lies at the heart of attempts to protect the unborn through legislation concerning voluntary termination of pregnancies and endeavours in the USA to criminalize certain 'unfit' states of motherhood such as drug-addiction or HIV infection.

Children in this image are not curbed nor beaten into submission, they are encouraged, enabled and facilitated. The formalization of the Apollonian child occurs with Rousseau; he is the author of their manifesto, *Émile*. It is in this work that Rousseau reveals the child's innate and immanent capacity for reason and he instructs us that they have natural virtues and dispositions which only require coaxing out into the open. Rousseau provides a rationale for the idea that children are born good, and beyond showing us that each child has a unique potential he states something completely new for its time and formative for the future – namely, that children are different from adults; they are an ontology in its own right and as such deserve special treatment and care.

Let us be clear, these two images of the child that I have designated as the Dionysian and the Apollonian are not literal descriptions of the way that children intrinsically differ; they are no more than images. Yet these images are immensely powerful, they live on and give force to the different discourses that we have about children; they constitute summaries of the way we have, over time, come to treat and process children 'normally'. What I am pointing to here is that these images are informative of the shifting strategies that Western society has exercised in its increasing need to control, socialize and constrain people in the transition towards modernity. As contexts of control they bear a striking resemblance to the 'positional' and the 'personal' generated in Bernstein's work.[38]

For this part of the analysis I shall draw on the work of Foucault[39] in his genealogy of discipline and punishment in modern society which, although not specifically about children, has profound implications for our changing ways of thinking about the child. What we have to keep in mind, however, is that such work is directing us away from explanations in terms of exterior structural forms and directing us towards the understanding of interiority. This is a point stressed by Steedman in her major thesis on the search for the internalized self through ideas of childhood, which she concludes as follows:

> The search is not the historian's alone. The search is for the self and the past that is lost and gone; and some of the ways in which, since the end of the eighteenth century, the lost object has come to assume the shape and form of the child.[40]

Foucault, whom we encountered in the last chapter, offers us a breakdown of the changes in what he calls the 'anatomy of power' in Western culture and a pivotal change occurs, he suggests, in the mid-eighteenth century – parallel with Rousseau's announcement of the modern child. What we are offered is a description of two images of discipline, which reflect two modes of control, which are, in turn, aspects of two forms of social integration shifting from an old European order to the new order of modern industrial society. These two images resonate strongly with my depictions of the Dionysian and the Apollonian child. Foucault sets out from the mode of imprisonment characteristic of the *ancien régime* in France, one rooted in the barbarities of medieval times, and proceeds to unravel the new penology of the post-Revolutionary state – a style of punishment that is premised on very different ideas concerning the appropriate nature of correction. The year 1789 did not provide an immediate and dramatic break in continuity, there was what might be described as a pre-paradigmatic stage of penology when the more advanced thinkers of the age set out to defame and undermine the old system of punishment and establish in its place a new system theorized much more in terms of dissuasion. The newly emergent methods of discipline show similarities with and influences from other areas of social life like, for example, the armed forces and the school system. So, as Sheridan pointed out, in relation to Foucault's thesis: 'there is an astonishing coincidence between the new prison and other contemporary institutions: hospital, factory, school and barracks'[41] and, for our purposes, regimes of child care.

Foucault's essay begins with an account of the appalling violence and degradation publicly inflicted on a man found guilty of attempting to murder King Louis XVth of France. It consists of plucking of the flesh, burning with oil and sulphur, dismembering and drawing-and-quartering. From this hyperbole of retributive punishment Foucault informs us that such awe-full spectacles diminish as we move into the nineteenth century. Through this historical period, it would seem, attention moves away from the execution of punishment to the mechanism of trial and sentence. In essence, the display of excessive symbolism is replaced by rational process. This transition in punishment is taken to reflect an overall change of collective attitudes into the form of society where there seems to be more kindness and, at least, an appearance of public humanism. This is matched by a diminution in brutality and a recognition of the impropriety of pain. In terms of judicial regimes this instances a transition from retribution to restitution. Violence against the physical body is gradually transformed into a more subtle and intrusive correction and training of the very soul. The government of the individual in modernity has moved from the outside to the inside. It will be recalled that Durkheim turned to an examination of judicial systems as indicators of the real but intangible forms of solidarity.

Clearly the implementation of discipline at the societal level cannot be random and spontaneous, it requires a number of concerted strategies to ensure a uniform application and result.

Primary among these is the exercise and manipulation of space. People are controlled in relation to the different spaces they inhabit; discipline works through the division and subdivision of action into spatial units. Think of children having a particular seat at the dinner table or in the car, being sent to their room, playing outside, going to school, attending assemblies, working in classes or gymnasia and, of course, being seated at desks, in rows, in groups or whatever. The 'reading corner' takes on a new significance. Foucault tells us that the original model for spatial control was the monastery cell or indeed the dungeon – this cellular metaphor extends out into other social institutions. The logistics of modernity turn masses of soldiers into lines of tents or barracks, factories become production lines with workers isolated by task within the division of labour, and hospitals become the classification of sickness on a ward system.

The other major strategy of control is temporal. The whole being of a child is delineated and paced according to a timetable. This too, Foucault tells us, is of monastic origin. The child's rising and sleeping, eating and entertainment are all prescribed in time. The very idea of a school curriculum is an organization of activities around a political economy of form in relation to content. What people learn is scheduled in relation to decisions about relevance and compulsion. The practice of being a child is marked out in stages, solidified and institutionalized by Piaget and conceptualized as 'development'. The implications of an individual's response to such an organization of time is critical to his/her placement in hierarchies of merit and achievement which ultimately relate to the existing system of social stratification and the distribution of life-chances in the wider society. Even the child's body is organized temporally in terms of its ablution, nutrition, excretion, exercise, etc., and all of this is homologous to the drilling that occurs in the armed forces and the specialization and division of labour on the factory floor. These are the modern ergonomics of fitting people to functions.

Power is organized through the combination of strategies, barrages of controlling mechanisms are arranged in tactics, subjects become objects to be gathered, transported and located through collective action. Foucault agrees, implicitly, with Durkheim before him, that the individual emerges from patterns of constraint. What Foucault adds to Durkheim's sociology is suspicion. It would appear then that the character of social structures provides for the possibility of personal expression. The individual, whether adult or child, when rendered object, itself becomes instrumental in the exercise of power – such is the force of ideology; the impersonal impact of partial ideas upon action. As Deleuze and Guattari[42] tell us, the modern nuclear family structure is one of the foremost devices for shaping the individual and restricting desire in capitalist societies, and it is psychoanalysis in adulthood that helps to reinforce that restraint.

Modern power does not exercise itself with the omnipotent symbolism of the scaffold; no longer are we witness to the excessive and triumphant zeal that was directed towards the Dionysian child. Modern power is calculating, it is suspicious and it always appears modest in its application. It operates through scopic regimes, through observation that is organized hierarchically, through judgements rendered normative within social structures and through scrutiny and examination. Observation has become a primary metaphor in the social sciences as it reflects the dominant form of the relations between people and certainly the relations between adults and the new, visible, Apollonian child. The crudity of the old regime of control in social relations gives way to the modern disciplinary apparatus, the post-Rousseau-nian way of looking at and monitoring the child in mind and body. Surveillance, in the form of child care, proliferates in its intensity and penetration through the agencies of midwives and health-visitors, nurses and doctors, post-natal clinics, schools and teachers, psychometric tests, examinations, educational psychology, counselling, social workers and so on and on through the layers of scrutiny and isolation; all constituted for the child's own good. In relation to the expanding 'gaze of the psychologist' Rose informed us that:

It was once the privilege of the wealthy, the noble, and the holy to have their individuality remarked upon, described, documented, recorded for posterity in image and text. But during the nineteenth century the individualizing gaze alighted upon those at the other end of power relations – the criminal, the madman, the pauper, the defective were to be the target of many laborious and ingenious projects to document their uniqueness, to record it and classify it, to discipline their difference. Children were to become favoured objects and targets of such programmes of individualization. Psychologists were to claim a particular expertise in the disciplining of the

uniqueness and idiosyncrasies of childhood, individualizing children by categorizing them, calibrating their apti-
tudes, inscribing their peculiarities in an ordered form,
managing their variability conceptually, and governing it
practically.[43]

The Apollonian child is truly visible; it is most certainly seen and
not heard.

Such a 'seeing' social structure Foucault epitomizes through
the symbol of the 'ideal prison' – namely, Jeremy Bentham's
sinister invention, the 'panopticon'. The panopticon, unlike the
more familiar 'star' prison, was circular with cells arranged in
layers of rings around a central observation tower. Each cell
would contain one isolated inmate, illuminated by natural lighting
from behind and at the front, wholly exposed, through the complete cage, to the constant gaze of the observation tower. The
surveillance from the observation tower takes place through slots
which are not illuminated from behind, thus the inmates of the
cells did not know when, or indeed if, they were being watched.
Effectively then, it was as if they were being watched all of the
time. One might properly suggest that the constant surveillance
became a feature of the prisoners' consciousness, a motive in
their demeanour and self-presentation; they grew to watch themselves. The panopticon presents itself at a variety of levels: first,
it as a built reality; second, symbolically it is the embodiment of
an ideal for maximizing scrutiny and control while minimizing
the response and intervention of those being controlled; and
finally it stands as an apt metaphor for the exercise of power in
modern society – in terms of our interests in this chapter: socialization, education, child care and provision. There is a delicacy and
a rapidity in the management of persons through panopticism.

CONCLUSION

In summary we might suggest that the Dionysian child is an
instance of a social structure where the rules and beliefs are
external and consensual: a society where people are less different
and it is the affirmation of their similarities that is at the basis of
their views on child-rearing. The offending, or evil, child has to
be beaten into submission; an external and public act that celebrates and reaffirms the shared values of their historical period.
Any transgression in the form of childish behaviour threatens the

very core of the collectivity. To be socialized is to become one with the normative social structure and so the idea of evil that is projected out into the image of the Dionysian child is, in fact, providing a vehicle for expunging all sentiments that threaten the sacred cohesion of the adult world. To this end, real children in such a society sacrifice their childhood to the cause of the collective adult good. As a result of such control the growing individual learns a respect for society through the experience of shame.

The Apollonian child, on the other hand, may be seen to occupy a social structure permeated by panopticism. The rules and beliefs are more diffuse, people are more different and isolated, and it is consequently more difficult for them to operate within a sense of shared values. Within such a world people manifest their uniqueness and children must be reared to express what is peculiarly special about their personalities. All of this difference is, of course, both volatile and subversive and must be policed if collective life is to be sustained at all. The control moves subtly in response to such a potentially fragmented social structure; as few symbols are shared, externality is an improper arena in which to uphold the sacred. Consequently the control moves inside, from the public to the private, and so we monitor and examine and watch the Apollonian child; he or she in turn learns to watch over themselves and shame is replaced by guilt. The panopticon dream is now complete through the internalization of surveillance in the formation of children's psyches. The Apollonian projection into childhood now appears as a way of resolving the loss of freedom and creativity in adult life.

Bernstein,[44] drawing on Durkheim's[45] analysis of simple and complex forms of social organization, had provided an earlier model for an examination of different kinds of relationship between adults and children in the form of different ways of organizing schooling. This, like the ideas of Foucault already discussed, is also instructive of different visions of society. Bernstein's work is most important in this context because he is precisely addressing the transition that has occurred in our image of the learner (the child) and treating it as indicative of changing standards of normality within modern society. In line with my conception of the Dionysian child and Foucault's conception of the *ancien régime* of punishment, Bernstein had already described the 'closed' curriculum and for the Apollonian child and panopticism, the 'open' curriculum. In the transition towards modernity from one form of schooling into another Bernstein tells us that there is a weakening of the symbolic significance and ritualization of punishment. Control in schools becomes more personalized, children are confronted more as individuals and there is a reduced appeal to shared loyalties. A child's activities are less likely to be prescribed by formal categories such as gender, IQ and age, but rather by the individual's needs and special qualities. There is a complementary alteration in the authority structure between adult and child, the teacher becomes a problem-poser and the authority resides within the learning material. Thus the act of learning through self-discovery celebrates choice and difference. Overall, the learning child has greater autonomy, higher levels of personal aspiration and more available choice. Bernstein concludes his analysis by saying that:

> None of this should be taken in the spirit that yesterday there was order today only flux. Neither should it be taken as a long sigh over the weakening of authority and its social basis. Rather we should be eager to explore changes in the forms of social integration in order to re-examine the basis of social control.[46]

This is a significant imperative for any sociological understanding of childhood, that the child is always revealing of the grounds of social control. Thus in one sense we get the children we deserve or, to put it more formally, our historical perspectives on normality in childhood reflect the changes in the organization of our social structure.

Therefore when Donzelot[47] tells us that the child has become the meeting place of the political contract and the psychological complex he is developing a wider argument about the functioning of control in modern life. The contemporary political state no longer addresses the polity as a whole but rather treats the family as its basic unit of control. All ideas and practices concerning the care of, justice for, and protection of the child can be seen to be instrumental in the ideological network that preserves the status quo. The 'tutelary complex' that Donzelot describes, is one that has become established through the practices of social workers and professional carers, and this complex intrudes into 'difficult' families but treads a careful line between repression and dependency such that the family is preserved as the unit of attention and the house of the child.

NOTES

[1] Isaac Bashevis Singer speech on receiving the Nobel Prize for literature, *The Observer*, 17 December 1978.

[2] J. Elshtain, *The Family in Political Thought*, Amherst: University of Massachusetts Press, 1982, p. 289.

[3] C. Jenks (ed.), *The Sociology of Childhood: Essential Readings*, London: Batsford, 1982 (reprinted Aldershot: Gregg, 1992).

[4] M. Douglas, 'Speech, class and Basil Bernstein' in *The Listener*, 9 March 1972.

[5] M. Mead and M. Wolfenstein, *Childhood in Contemporary Cultures*, Chicago: Chicago University Press, 1954, p. 3.

[6] M. Hoyles, *Changing Childhood*, London: Writers and Readers Pub. Coop., 1979, p. 16.

[7] V. Zelizer, *Pricing the Priceless Child: The Changing Value of Children*, New York: Basic Books, 1985.

[8] M. Hoyles, op. cit., p. 23.

[9] C. Jenks, 'Social theorizing and the child: constraints and possibilities' in S. Doxiadis (ed.), *Early Influences Shaping the Individual*, NATO Advanced Studies Workshop, London: Plenum, 1989.

[10] H. Cunningham, *The Children of the Poor: Representations of Childhood since the Seventeenth Century*, Oxford: Blackwell, 1991, p. 7.

[11] W. Stainton-Rogers, D. Hevey and E. Ash (eds), *Child Abuse and Neglect: Facing the Challenge*, London: Open University, 1989, p. 54.

[12] C. Steedman, *Childhood, Culture and Class in Britain: Margaret McMillan 1860–1931*, London: Virago, 1990, pp. 63–64.

[13] P. Ariès, *Centuries of Childhood*, London: Cape, 1962.

[14] Ibid., p. 395.

[15] Ibid., p. 31.

[16] Ibid., p. 125.

[17] I. Illich, *Deschooling Society*, Harmondsworth: Penguin, 1973, p. 33.

[18] C. Steedman, op. cit., p. 62.

[19] P. Robertson, 'Home as a nest: middle class childhood in nineteenth century Europe' in L. DeMause (ed.), *The History of Childhood*, London: Souvenir, 1976, p. 407.

[20] H. Cunningham, op. cit., p. 43.

[21] For critiques of Ariès' thesis see L. Pollock, *Forgotten Children*, Cambridge: Cambridge University Press, 1983; J. Kroll, 'The concept of childhood in the Middle Ages' in *Journal of the History of Behavioral Sciences*, vol. 13, no. 4, 1977, pp. 384–393; D. Stannard, 'Death and the Puritan child' in *American Quarterly*, no. 26, 1974, pp. 456–476; R. Beales, 'In search of the historical child: miniature adulthood and youth in colonial New England' in *American Quarterly*, no. 27, 1975, pp. 379–398; A. Macfarlane, *The Origins of English Individualism. The Family, Property and Social Transition*, Cambridge: Cambridge University Press, 1979; B. Hanawalt, 'Childrearing among the lower classes of late medieval England' in *Journal of Interdisciplinary History*, vol. 8, no. 1, 1977, pp. 1–22; P. Laslett and R. Wall (eds), *Household and Family in Past Times*, Cambridge: Cambridge University Press, 1972; D. Hunt, *Parents and Children in History*, New York: Harper-Row, 1972; A. Wilson, 'The infancy of the history of childhood: an appraisal of Phillipe Ariès' in *History and Theory*, vol. 19, 1980, pp. 132–154.

[22] L. Pollock, op. cit., p. 64.

[23] L. DeMause, op. cit.

[24] Ibid., p. 1.

[25] E. Shorter, *The Making of the Modern Family*, London: Collins, 1976.

[26] Ibid.

[27] N. Rose, *Governing the Soul: The Shaping of the Private Self*, London: Routledge, 1989.

[28] C. Jenks, 1989, op. cit.

[29] J. Hillman, *Loose Ends*, New York: Spring Publications, 1975, p. 8.

[30] E. Durkheim, *Moral Education*, New York: Free Press, 1961.

[31] P. Bourdieu and J.-C. Passeron, *Reproduction: In Education, Society and Culture*, London: Sage, 1977.

[32] G. Boas, *The Cult of the Child*, London: Warburg, 1966.

[33] J. Rose, 'State and language: Peter Pan as written for the child' in C. Steedman, C. Urwin and V. Walkerdine (eds), *Language, Gender and Childhood*, London: Routledge & Kegan Paul, 1985, p. 88.

[34] M. Shipman, *Childhood: A Sociological Perspective*, Slough: NFER, 1972.

[35] P. Coveney, *Poor Monkey*, London: Rockcliff, 1957.

[36] Ibid., pp. 31–32.

[37] A. Millar, *Thou Shalt Not Be Aware: Society's Betrayal of the Child*, London: Pluto Press, 1990, p. 5.
[38] B. Bernstein, *Class, Codes and Control*, vol. 1, London: Routledge & Kegan Paul, 1974.
[39] M. Foucault, *Discipline and Punish*, London: Allen Lane, 1977.
[40] C. Steedman, *Strange Dislocations: Children and the Idea of Human Interiority 1780–1930*, London: Virago, 1995, p. 174.
[41] A. Sheridan, *Michel Foucault: The Will to Truth*, London: Tavistock, 1980.
[42] G. Deleuze and F. Guattari, *Anti-Oedipus*, New York: Viking, 1983.
[43] N. Rose, op. cit., p. 132.
[44] B. Bernstein, 'Open schools, open society' in *Class, Codes and Control*, vol. 3., London: Routledge & Kegan Paul, 1975.
[45] E. Durkheim, *The Division of Labour in Society*, New York: Free Press, 1964.
[46] B. Bernstein, 1975, op. cit.
[47] J. Donzelot, *The Policing of Families*, London: Hutchinson, 1986.

4

The abuse of childhood

We might rightly suppose that children have been and will continue to be a constant component of human society. Individuals and collectivities reproduce themselves both biologically and culturally and children are practical embodiments of these processes. Children constitute the perpetual renewal of human relations. They are encoded bio-genetically but also imbued with social values and cultural capital through early socialization and formal education.[1] Children are a concrete presence with needs, demands, dispositions and a burgeoning intentionality, but they also comprise analytic trajectories in terms of the psychological projections and collective expectations of the larger, and more powerful, adult group within society. The former is a world created for them through their 'natural' character and the latter a world constrained for them through their 'social' status. The latter is the world that we refer to as 'childhood'.

The vast body of literature written with a concern for the history of childhood, partly reviewed and analysed in the previous chapter, indicates that the socio-cultural context within which the 'natural' child has lived through the ages has varied considerably.[2] The phenomenological outcome of this well-documented diachronic instability has been that childhood itself has not been a constant within the historical process. As a social status childhood has come to be variously recognized and understood through its apprehension in routinely emergent collective perceptions that are grounded in changing politics, philosophy, economics, social policy or whatever. Such knowledge is a central feature of this chapter, we must envision the child within a broad cultural context.

The written history of childhood is a territory well charted and populated with persuasive ideas that have, in many senses, burdened us with a vision of the child through modernity that has overwhelmed our capacity to theorize the child in the rapidly transforming conditions of late-modernity. This is an unfortunate consequence in two ways: first, because we all might tend to operate with an outmoded and inappropriate set of expectations and demands on today's child as an existential practice,[3] and second, because we are unreflexive concerning our own relationship with childhood and the compound set of issues in regard to our own individual self-identity, our shared senses of collective value, and our general appreciation of the condition of late-modern society.

AN INCREASE IN CHILD ABUSE?

This chapter is concerned to initiate the articulation of a new and different vision of the child; however, it sets out from a modern social problem. This is the problem of child abuse that we now recognize as an intensively documented aspect of the contemporary practical relationship between adults and children. More specifically then, my starting point is the seemingly unprecedented increase in child abuse in Western societies over the last three decades. Such abuse is not singular in its manifestations, which include physical,[4] sexual[5] and psychological or emotional[6] forms, its etiologies are manifold and its impact on the individually engaged personalities is complex, in every sense. In this chapter, however, I realize 'abuse' as a unitary phenomenon for I am interested in the nature of our collective responses to it rather than in the construction of a morphology of its types or in the production of a causal analysis to account for its occurrence.[7] To this end I attempt an examination of the application and meaning of the very idea of 'abuse' within modern discourses about childhood; that is, I investigate its intentional or purposive character.

In this sense actual child abuse is only the beginning of our real topic and the kernel of my theoretical interest in child abuse is the current collective upsurge of interest in it. Finkelhor had prefigured this perspective in his work, specifically on sexual abuse, when he wrote:

> Whenever a social problem appears suddenly, and of great magnitude, we are apt to wonder why. More than any other social problem in recent memory, sexual abuse has risen precipitously in public awareness from virtual obscurity to extreme high visibility. Why has this emergence been so dramatic?[8]

What I suggest then, is that the phenomenon of child abuse has emerged as a malign and exponential growth towards the conclusion of the twentieth century not because of any significant alteration in the pattern of our behaviour towards children but because of the changing patterns of personal, political and moral control in social life more generally which have, in turn, affected our vision of childhood. Whereas an antique vision of the child rendered abuse unseen or unintelligible, modernity illuminated mistreatment and highlighted the necessity of care. However, the late-modern, emergent vision of the child, discussed here, brings abuse into prominence through scrutiny and surveillance[9] but also through the peculiar structural demands on the constitution of personal identity and social relationships wrought through accelerative social change.

THE MYTHOLOGY OF CHILD ABUSE

The mythology of child abuse must surely begin with the story of Medea. Her grisly legend, as conveyed by Euripides and by Seneca, is instructive of the shock and outrage expressed, both publicly and privately, in response to the spectrum of damage that has been inflicted upon children, by adults, from antiquity up until the present day. It is instructive further in relation to the intelligibility of such abhorrent acts as emanating not so much from devils and stereotypical perverts as from members of that same outraged public . . . real people.

Medea, a sorceress, who having aided Jason in his quest to obtain the Golden Fleece, became his consort and, subsequently, mother of their two sons. Jason later abandoned her and she, in a ferocious state of negative passion, burned down their palace, murdered the King of Corinth and the princess, her rival, and then fled to Athens with her own children whom she ritualistically slaughtered en route. This catalogue of carnage and destruction was not, tragically enough, directed specifically at its subjects but rather at Jason for his betrayal. A nemesis with its victim at one remove; the immediate sufferers being secondary to the noumenon of the act, but suffering supremely, nevertheless. This resonates with the diffuse, and often unintended, consequences wrought through the exercise of modern forms of social control.

The classical point of this moral tale is to express the potential magnitude of a woman's desire for revenge; so consuming that she could overcome her maternal drives and kill her own offspring. One point that I wish to extrapolate from this fable is the recognition of, though not justification for, the human possibility of transcending the 'natural', or rather transgressing the 'cultural',[10] that appears to have become utterly routine in the commission of acts of child abuse in contemporary society.

Progressive society provides us with few reasons for indignation, the child abuser, we might suggest, is the last domestic variety. All 'decent' and 'right-thinking' people know that adults regard childhood as a state of dependency that we relate to through strategies of care. Physical, sexual and psychological abuse have no part in either the moral or the material contexts of adult–child relationships. The invocation of the normative assumptions inherent in the notions of 'decency' and 'right-mindedness' is a deliberate device to open up their ideological connotations that I shall latterly expand.

Medea's story tells us two other things that I will also subsequently develop: first, that child abuse is nothing new, it has always been an immanent feature of the relationship between adults and the young, concretely the potential resides within the differentials of both power and status. Thus, despite the fact that modern paediatric history would have us believe that Freud invented childhood sexuality at the end of the nineteenth century, that the recommended repression of the twentieth century had driven it underground and that we, collectively, have re-invented it in the face of the coming *fin de siècle*, it will be my contention that childhood libido, along with the innocence and the evil of children have all, in an analytic rather than any positivistic sense, always been with us – just as has adult usage. The erotic in child–adult relationships has been newly articulated in relation to the axes of purity and danger though, as Freud discovered, it has never been a dimension of human experience that dares to speak its name too loudly:

> Naturally the main opprobrium fell on his [Freud's] assertion that children are born with sexual urges, which undergo a complicated development before they attain the familiar adult form, and that their first sexual objects are their parents. This assault on the pristine innocence of childhood was unforgivable. In spite of the contemporary furore and abuses, however, which continued for perhaps twenty years, time worked its way with the book, and Freud's prediction that its conclusions would before long be taken for granted is approaching fulfilment.[11]

Second, and in line with the ideas of the social constructionists,[12] the hermeneutic fecundity of Medea's story, which I have already constituted as instancing 'abuse' and/or 'revenge', enables us to reveal the socially contexted and historically semantic character of this phenomenon, and indeed, any other social phenomenon. This is no slight attempt to depotentiate or trivialize the life-damaging trauma that can so often stem from the experience of 'abuse' in its variety of manifestations, but rather a careful examination of the application and meaning of the very idea of 'abuse' within modern discourses about childhood, that is, its intentional character. Thus, as I have already stated, a large part of my theoretical interest in child abuse is the current collective upsurge of interest in child abuse.

This discursive myth of Medea from which I begin, and the codes that it sets, require unscrambling but not, however, with the confidence that might seem to suggest that such a complex and confusing phenomenon as current-day child abuse can be simply explained. Let us now relocate our encoded concerns within the current myth, that is, the unprecedented explosion in the occurrence of child abuse in Western culture over the last three decades. The sustained application of the concept of myth here is in no sense meant to prejudge or diminish the phenomenon. The concept is reinvoked not as a concrete description of a fictitious story but in the anthropological sense of defining the cultural process, in narrative form, by which a society attempts to render meaningful and coherent the relationship between existing cosmologies and emergent behavioural anomalies. So what are the conventional explanations of the recent 'given' increase, and well-documented increase, in cases of child abuse?

CONTEMPORARY EXPLANATIONS OF CHILD ABUSE

What is clearly true is that a vastly increasing number of cases of child abuse are reported now than was the case thirty, or even twenty, years ago. This primarily indicates a conceptual and methodological discrepancy between 'incidence' and prevalence'.[13] However the increase was, at its inception, viewed by many commentators as a social trend, and initial explanations for this apparent trend were sadly simplistic, a weakness stemming from the face-value positivism at the heart of their grasp of the issue. The face-value explanations are almost universally short-term, they are synchronic and hold synchronic homologies with the phenomenon itself – they refer largely to the modern nuclear family, its transfiguration and the threats to its inherent stability. They are interesting in a variety of ways, both analytic and ideological, but also when read in relation to work by Ferguson, albeit writing in another context, who stated that:

> However exaggerated or oversimplified the claims of a generation of sociologists directly linking the 'emergence' of the modern nuclear family with the rise of the bourgeoisie may be, there seems little doubt that the image of childhood has undergone significant changes during the development of capitalism.[14]

The explanations to which I refer are relatively dispersed in their origins but succinctly assembled by Finkelhor,[15] even though it is clear that he does not necessarily agree with them or their implications for social policy and social change. The primary point would seem to stem from a 'functionalist' position, or what has been referred to elsewhere as a 'New Rightist' view of the family.[16] The argument notes and bewails the seemingly rapid deterioration and enfeeblement of the connubial bond over the last thirty years. What, it is noted, accompanies such a withering, is not a disillusionment with partnering relationships so much as a relentless and relatively uncommitted domestic mobility. People change partners more readily and more often. This means, in turn, that children are more subject to the close and continued company of step-fathers and boyfriends while simultaneously unprotected by the incest taboo, but also children are routinely party to the conflicts and strains that accompany either the forging of new relationships or the breakdown of those already established. With the shift in this affective centre of modern social life, it is argued, children become less integrated through care and thus subject to higher risk from all forms of abuse.

Parallel with the preceding explanation is the widely held view that the moral, or rather the sexual, climate has altered in modern Western societies since the 1960s. A consequence, and purpose, of this much vaunted period of recent history was the supposed liberalization of collective constraint and individual attitude towards sexual practices. The impact of such a process, it has been claimed, is the diffusion of standards constituting proper sexual conduct and the erosion of the conventional authority behind previously exercised sexual prohibitions. Although much is made through everyday folklore and the mass media about the fixity and the proprietal character of the practices of the past age (and one suspects that this is not the unique province of the generation straddling the 1960s 'sexual revolution'), it is a vast step to proposing a causal relation with, rather than a correlation or elective affinity with, or at most an aggravation of, the problem of child abuse. It is an argument as tenuous as, and indeed of the same order as, that which regards rape as being instigated by pornography.

Finally, an extension of the preceding argument, and one also reviewed by Finkelhor, is that the 1960s also created an ungrounded and thus unrealistic anticipation, on the part of individuals, of a higher level and greater intensity of sexual activity. Such raised expectations, faced with the reality of an unaltered state of availability of willing sexual partners may, it is supposed, divert the falsely inflated desires of some men to the more pliant and subservient object provided by the child.

Much of this psycho-sociological speculation takes the problem as given, the phenomenon as short-term and local and the explanation as available, and readily so, at the level of attitude.

Let us now begin to expand and problematize our topic and place it, more relatively and, I would suggest, more instructively, within the context of changing social structures. Let us, then, set out from a childhood historicity.

THE EVOLUTION OF THE CHILD AND CHILD ABUSE

In the last chapter we saw that Ariès, DeMause, Shorter and a whole corpus of, what I am referring to as, post- or neo-Enlightenment historians have generated accounts of the evolution of childhood status that share certain tenets. These tenets are: (a) that once childhood as a category of persons was not part of society's collective perceptions; (b) that childhood and patterns of child care have evolved into being; (c) that such an evolution has harnessed our affections for children but has been directed by the advancement of ideas in relation to philosophies of human nature, theories of education, economies of human capital, and the politics of human rights; (d) that the emotional, physical and psychological needs of children are increasingly well taken care of; and (e) that overall, the experience of childhood in contemporary society supersedes all previous historical manifestations.

What none of these accounts provides is any explanation for the unprecedented occurrence of child abuse in modern Western society. Indeed, if the logic of their arguments were to achieve its telos then our very topic would have disappeared. Their analytic gradient tilting us into modernity rests on a Darwinian aggregate of evolution, growth, visibility, improvement, achievement and rectitude. The only possible explanation for modern child abuse within such a framework would be utterly individualistic, not conceivably an inherent feature of modern social structures, but rather gross individual psycho-pathology or forms of atavism – that is, explanation through the devices of the stereotypical 'pervert' or 'molester' which common sense so readily brings to mind. The kind of creature emerging from such an explanation would be so unrecognizable in our scale of social types that we even permit its placement lowest within hierarchies of pathology – for example, Rule 43 prisoners, the 'nonces' within the British penal system, the sexual offenders nominally segregated but practically prey to the sustained harassment and violence of staff and inmates alike, with the implicit approval of all.

This is, of course, no more than a convenient displacement of the problem and simply not true. The vast majority of child abusers are parents, step-parents, siblings or trusted kin,[17] the evidence suggesting that this covers between 75 and 90 per cent of all recorded cases. So we are not seeking explanation in terms of occasional, random occurrences or shadowy, hyperbolic figures of evil, rather we are seeking the routine and the commonplace – the normal type of people who have mundane relationships with children. It is not public parks and crawling cars that are the primary source of threat to the child, but the family. The family is one of the most dangerous places for children to live in.[18]

The analytic gradient has to be levelled, it cannot be that once there were no distinguishable children, now the world is organized in relation to children, that once abuse of people was rife, now abuse of children is unthinkable. Rather I would argue that child abuse is not an original event, there has never been a historical period nor a particular society in which children were not exploited, sexually molested and subjected to physical and psychological violence.[19] It might be plausible to argue, adopting a long-term historical view, that abuse is declining rather than increasing, that it is better to have been a child in Thatcher's Britain than in that of Dickens, or a child of modern Western Europe than of antiquity in Asia. However, the point remains, child abuse is neither a thing of the past nor is it original – it is a constant feature of human social relations. Freeman[20] argued similarly that abuse is rooted in our earliest myths and history. He produces a socio-legal chronology of the benchmarks in child protection such as the 1883 Report of Commissioners on Employment of Children in Factories which deplored the cruel attitudes and practices of adult workers towards their younger colleagues and made recommendations for positive reform. However, changes and innovations such as these, he suggested, may have appeared to benefit children but have not necessarily meant a decline in the level of child abuse. No evidence that he points to is sufficient to convince us that child abuse is less prevalent today than it has been in previous epochs. Freeman further concluded that the 'discovery' of child abuse as a social problem in more recent years is not necessarily attributable to an increase in abuse itself.

Kempe, an American paediatrician with an established research record in this field (indeed he is often referred to as 'the discoverer' or, rather more ironically, 'the founding father' of child abuse), concurs with the view that child abuse is a perennial feature of human societies. When, in the 1960s, radiologists in certain American hospitals began to publish reports on bone fractures in young children that were either not accounted for or inadequately explained by their parents, it was Kempe who generated the concept of the 'battered baby' and began to make public the syndrome of child abuse. The 'battered baby' became transformed, in the less-accusatory parlance of the British social services, into the 'non-accidental injury', but it was, and remained, Kempe's formulation of a new category of social problem that prevailed. The 'new-ness' of the problem took on a different and more subtle form when Kempe drew a distinction between changing social practices and changing social perceptions in relation to child abuse.

> A book on child abuse could not have been written one hundred years ago. If an investigator from the 1970s were to be transported back to the 19th century so he could survey the family scene with modern eyes, child abuse would be clearly visible to him. In the past, however, it was largely invisible to families and their communities. Before it could be acknowledged as a social ill, changes had to occur in the sensibilities and outlook of our culture.[21]

So from the 'invention' of child abuse in the 1960s Kempe's position seems to transform into a 'dis-covery' of child abuse in the 1970s. The prevalence of child abuse as a social practice, far from spontaneously re-generating in the second half of the twentieth century, had, in fact, been constant, which is testified to by Kempe's renewed interest in the historical dimension of the phenomenon.[22] However, the incidence of child abuse during that period, in terms of reported and recorded occurrence, was to be treated as a novel phenomenon, an expanding phenomenon, and a phenomenon worthy of further explanation in itself.

In many senses we can now see that Kempe has much in common with the post-Rousseaunian optimism concerning the child shared by Ariès, DeMause and Shorter. He is not, however, insisting that our practices in relation to children have become necessarily more refined and less abusive, but that our social attitudes towards children in general have become more alert, caring and loving. What follows from this is that as a collectivity we are more watchful and attentive to the nurture, protection and well-being of our young. It is not essentially that the character or pattern of our actions towards children has altered but that our threshold of tolerance of potentially 'abusive' conduct has lowered, in the same way that yesterday's sexual banter between men and women has become, through a shift in perspective, today's sexual harassment. Now such a lowering of our tolerance, a shift in perspective, does not usually come about at random or through the desires of the people at large, it is usually driven. The forces behind such a switch are the discourses that politicize events and have the power to transform previously held cultural configurations. These forces are primarily intellectual, but eventually governmental and, through the mediation of social policy and legislation, such forces eventually become dispersed and accepted, or 'normalized', in everyday language. As Foucault has stated in relation to incest:

> Incest was a popular practice, and I mean by this, widely practised among the populace, for a very long time. It was towards the end of the 19th century that various social pressures were directed against it. And it is clear that the great interdiction against incest is an invention of the intellectuals. . . . If you look for studies by sociologists or anthropologists of the 19th century on incest you won't find any. Sure, there were some scattered medical reports and the like, but the practice of incest didn't really seem to pose a problem at the time.[23]

THE POLITICIZATION OF CHILD ABUSE

Clearly, as has been cited by Mayes *et al.*,[24] the two primary agencies engaged in the politicization of child abuse were both the Women's Movement and the child protection movement. Both groups were ultimately instrumental in instigating change in relation to public awareness and professional practice, even though both groups formulated the issue of abuse in very different ways and proposed very different remedies.

The child protection lobby tended to promote accounts in terms of family dysfunction, theories traceable to Parsonian systems theory. Here the basic model was that of the homeostatic unit generating social stability through the allocation and maintenance of roles, and psychological stability through the satisfaction of need-dispositions. An explanation of abuse might occur in relation to the failure of appropriate allocation or satisfaction, thus within such a holistic explanatory mode all members of a family were potentially complicit in the exercise of abusive practice.[25] So, for example, a spouse's withdrawal from sexual activity with their partner might divert anger or desire towards the children. The alternative, or often supplementary, mode of explanation within the child protection movement was that in terms of a 'cycle of abuse'. Here, emanating from an essentially behaviouristic model, it was argued that the abused grow up to practise abuse, indeed they become skilled abusers. The theorizing within the child protection movement sanctified the family and a view of the necessary role of the properly patterned relationship between men and women in promoting a healthy and thriving environment for the child. As a consequence it tended to recommend the preservation of the family through remedial therapy. What it also achieved was a shift in focus from the victim to the abuser and thus also made available the possibility of directing attention, if not blame, towards the mother. The politics of the child protection movement were essentially rooted in the conservation of the existing social order and as such it contained no concerted analysis of power relations within that order.

It was precisely this last omission that was the point of leverage for the women's movement. Across a variety of feminisms child abuse became identifiable as part of a continuum of male violence. Families were analysed in terms of two axes of power, namely gender and age – the vast majority of abusers were found to be men. The patriarchy thesis burgeoned, it was argued that there exists within modern Western society a dominant ideology of male supremacy and that the organization of families, accepted patterns of socialization, the occupational structure and the very formation of identity are regulated in relation to it. Child abuse could be seen then, as an instance of the patriarchal maintenance of social relations.[26] Sexual abuse is nothing more, nor less, than rape[27] and is like all forms of abuse in that they flow largely, it was argued, from men and are to be interpreted as a necessary accompaniment to the secondary status that is ascribed to both women and children within the culture. Rather than seeking to conserve the family such feminist arguments were far more radical in terms of recommending a dissolution of the existing order, as well as the protection of victims and the criminalization of abusers:

> Turning the earlier sociological discussions on their head, therefore, feminists argue that it is not the incest prohibition but, rather, the actual occurrence of incest which provides a key to a sociological understanding of social structure and culture.[28]

Corby,[29] writing to produce a theoretical basis for our understandings of child abuse rather than adding to the available repertoire of 'quick-fix' solutions that the urgency of child-protection practice demands through day-to-day pragmatics, provided an interesting account of the recent political history and policy context of the phenomenon. He stated that:

> child abuse is not a new phenomenon.... Nevertheless,
> fresh attempts to tackle child mistreatment are usually
> accompanied by the declaration that it is a new and as
> yet undiscovered problem. This 'newness' is seen as an
> important part of the process of establishing it as an issue
> requiring resources to tackle it. Often what is new about
> the problem is the way in which it is being defined or
> interpreted. This in turn can be linked to wider issues
> and concerns in society.[30]

While not wholly agreeing with the materialist reduction at the
heart of this passage I fully concur with the acknowledged persist-
ence of the phenomenon, with the idea that its topicalization is
a hermeneutic issue, and with the structuralist assertion that
such a reinterpretation is bound through homology with the wider
network of configurations that make up the society.

Williams[31] has stated that the quality of our system of education, and by implication our child-rearing practices, reflect upon
the quality of our culture. I would certainly hold to the view
that the texture of adult–child relationships in any historical
period can be seen as indicative of the condition of the social
bond. Bronfenbrenner took this position as axiomatic in the opening of his important, and surprising, 'coldwar' thesis on the *Two
Worlds of Childhood* when he said:

> How can we judge the worth of a society? On what basis
> can we predict how well a nation will survive and pros-
> per? Many indices could be used for this purpose, among
> them the Gross National Product, the birth rate, crime
> statistics, mental health data etc. In this book we propose
> yet another criterion: the concern of one generation for
> the next. If the children and youth of a nation are
> afforded opportunity to develop their capacities to the
> fullest, if they are given the knowledge to understand
> the world and the wisdom to change it, then the prospect
> is bright. In contrast, a society which neglects its children,
> however well it may function in other respects, risks even-
> tual disorganization and demise.[32]

We need then to attend seriously to this phenomenon of suppos-
edly increasing child abuse in as much as that it refers to the
wider state of the society. If the child is an icon of the condition
of the social structure at any particular time, and thus currently

emblematic of our collective responses to the impact of late-modernity, how do we seek to explain the increased attention paid to the abuse of today's children in relation to the altered circumstances of late-modern society?

THE CHILD IN MODERNITY – 'FUTURITY'

Both as professional social scientists and also as members of the lay public we are now very much aware of the impact that child protectionists and feminists have had upon our thinking about the child – but is that so, has child abuse not rather become symbolic of other things? In the same way that Medea was practising revenge, effectively stabbing at Jason 'through' their children, child protectionists are upholding the family and feminists are attacking male power. The child, in this instance as the recipient of abuse, can be seen as revealing of the grounds of social control.[33] Therefore when Donzelot[34] describes the child as the interface between politics and psychology he is producing the child as a metaphor for the strategies and functioning of control in modern life. The contemporary state no longer addresses the polity directly, governmentality like the discourse of morality has become oblique, the family is now the basic unit of control. All ideas and practices concerning the care of, justice for, and protection of the child can be seen to be instrumental in the ideological network that preserves the going order. The 'tutelary complex' that Donzelot describes, is one that has become established through the politicization of child abuse, for example, and institutionalized through the routine practices of social workers and professional carers. This complex, masked in the form of care and concern, intrudes into 'difficult' families but treads a careful line between repression and dependency such that the family is preserved as the unit of attention, for the dispersal of mechanisms of control, and also the house of the child.

The historical liberation of the child from adulthood, argued for by Ariès and others, may simply have rendered abuse less visible, or considerably more subtle. The freeing of the child from adult identity has not freed the child from adult society, instead it has led to the necessity of its constraint by collective practices. The obvious visibility and high profile of children in our contemporary patterns of relationship has made them subject to new forms of control.

This control, or governing, is both concrete and analytic. We actively govern real children, just as described, but we also handle, massage and manipulate images of children in, it could be suggested, abusive ways, either consciously or unconsciously, to achieve ends wildly in excess of particular, embodied children. I am thinking here of a range of phenomena as discrepant as pornography, advertising, children's fashion, the 1981 International Year of the Child, the Dutch parliament lowering the age of consent from 16 to 12 in 1990, the UK Government introducing a National Curriculum in state schools during 1988, and the extraordinary reportage of and response to alleged 'ritualistic Satanic abuse' in the British Isles during 1990 and so on. Just as the delineation of the child's particularity has given rise to specially fashioned forms of control so also has the diminution of public ignorance towards the child introduced new and intrusive forms of symbolic violence, extending from neurotic families[35] and parental sexual abuse, to commercial exploitation and projections of national identity. The child has become emblematic.

Child abuse is real, but it is equally a device for constituting a reality. As Stainton Rogers has pointed out: 'Social problems like child abuse are not things that happen but rather are ways of making sense'.[36] But this revelation is not the end of the issue, it is the beginning of the real issue. We started out from a myth and proceeded to a newer myth concerning the apparent epidemic of child abuse in contemporary Western culture. Why has child abuse recently become 'a way of making sense' of such vivid dimensions?

Let me unpack some of these assertions and then attempt to analyse what I see as the new liminality of the post-modern child. First, where did the modern child arise from? It was Rousseau who promulgated the manifesto of the child in modernity through *Émile* (1762), with its immanent, idealist, rational characteristics. Since that time Western society, it is generally supposed, has not looked back. Rousseau forged an uncontestable link between our understanding of the child and the emotions of the heart. He announced that humankind is naturally good and that it is only the constraints implicit in certain social structures or the corruption of some forms of social institutions that renders it bad. Children, who Rousseau regarded as the bearers of this 'goodness' in a primal condition, were to be educated properly and socialized according to 'natural' principles. Rousseau's 'savage' (a being wholly without the anthropological connotations of primitiveness), is a child highly charged with dispositions to love and to learn, and equipped with the propensity to become a good spouse, parent and citizen. Such an ideal being, the very image of modernity's child, is a stranger to avarice and is imbued with a natural altruism and kindliness. More than this, Rousseau's already overburdened creature is simultaneously the repository of all necessary wisdom. This child embodies an affective certainty which need not answer to objective, external criteria, and which is further insulated from scrutiny by Rousseau's implicit relativism and thus privatization of beliefs. We witness here the distillation of the principle of 'care' governing the modern relationship between adults and children but more than this we see the inauguration of the powerful commitment to childhood in Western society as a form of 'promise': a 'promise' of unimagined action, but also an extension of our own plans and a hedge against our own action as yet incomplete. Such a commitment has, for several generations, enabled us to indulge in pleasant reveries concerning tomorrow.

Once, it is assumed, we were unutterably beastly towards children,[37] at one time we did not attend to their specificity and difference at all,[38] and for whole epochs we routinely abandoned them.[39] But following the optimistic illumination of the Enlightenment children have become our principal concern, we have become their protectors and nurturers and they have become our primary love objects, our human capital and our future.

All of the neo-Enlightenment histories of infancy and maturation, only some of which we have reviewed, attest to this grand conceit, their analyses encourage our modern complacencies by regarding the archaeology of child-rearing with a disdainful backward glance. The brevity, ignorance, brutality and general ugliness of antiquity's parenting, we imagine, has been supplanted by a vision and attitude which has become crystallized into the form of a rational machine for nurture, the family and its macrocosm, the state. The modern family has become the locus for the confluence of politics and individual psychology, but beyond this it has emerged as both the primary unit for and also the site of governmentality, that is, it both absorbs and, in turn, distributes social control.

Through modernity childhood has gradually sequestered adult experience, it has claimed a greater duration within the total life experience, it has usurped and assumed greater and yet greater segments of adult labour: cognitive, affective and manual. Beyond this childhood has absorbed increased material provision and it has established this patterning of acquisitions as a 'natural' right policed by an ideology of care, grounded unassailably in the emotions. Adults (though primarily women) 'sacrifice everything' for their children and they, in return, are expected to experience 'the best time of their lives'. Adults have relinquished this space and this power in relation to a strictly moral dimension epitomized through the concept of 'dependency', but this, perhaps, disguises motivations of optimism, investment, and even a contemporary re-working of Weber's 'salvation anxiety'. Parental love and benevolent adult paternalism in general are not in question here, but rather the forms of social structure that accelerate their intensity and expand their currency. It is no great leap to see the absolute necessity and centrality of the modern nuclear family as the pivotal social space in this system of socialization.

The organization of this patterning of relationships and the emergence of a quasi superiority in the affectual attitude has, of course, not occurred in isolation, nor simply through the grand inspiration of Rousseau's romantic vision. The reconstruction of human relationality into the architecture of the modern family has been a recognizable compliment to the division of labour through industrialization, not cynically planned, but not 'naturally' evolved either. The modern family has become the basic unit of social cohesion in advancing capitalism, and though loving and supportive in its self-image it has become the very epitome of the rational enterprise. Families are cellular, mobile, manageable and accessible to emergent forms of mass communication, unlike the extended families that preceded them. They are also self-sustaining, self-policing, discrete yet wholly public in their orientation and, as I stated at the outset of this chapter, both biologically and culturally reproductive. They are a major component in the exercise of the contemporary principles of adaptation and integration; they are instrumental in their rationality by facilitating change while demonstrating stability to their members.

The modern family enabled the modern state to invest in 'futures'. The ideology of care both lubricated and legitimized the investment of economic and cultural capital in the 'promise' of childhood. Childhood is transformed into a form of human capital which, through modernity, has been dedicated to futures. The metaphoricity through which the discourse of childhood speaks is predicated on the absent presence of a desired tomorrow; with 'growth', 'maturation' and 'development' writ large at the level of individual socialization, and 'pools of ability' and a concern with the 'wastage of talent' at the level of formal state socialization. As children, and by way of children, we have, through modernity, dreamt of futures, and in so doing we have both justified and sought justification for modernity's expansionist urges in the post-Darwinian conflation of growth and progress.

The extant vision of childhood through the nineteenth and twentieth centuries had become one of 'futurity', and the much vaunted accretion of a 'caring', 'helping', 'enabling', 'facilitating' mode of nurture instances both the explicit awakening of a collective attitude more sensitive to children's needs, but also an implicit recognition of their worth and thus appropriate usage. The apparent gradual diminution of child abuse through the nineteenth century and on into the twentieth century can be seen as a considered shift from immediate to deferred gratification on the part of an increasingly enlightened adult society.

THE CHILD IN POST-MODERNITY – 'NOSTALGIA'

I now continue to view our phenomenon in the context of wider structural changes. Just as modern patterns of consumption have outstripped nineteenth-century economics, the late-modern division of labour and its accompanying social structures have mutated beyond the communities and solidarities described by classical sociology. Thus everyday late-modern modes of relationality have outgrown the mid-twentieth-century nuclear family. Things are not as they used to be and this is not a consequence of the erosion of the family, although this is what the rhetoric of contemporary politics often suggests in a variety of attempts to divert the level of problematic from the global and national to the local, and indeed the personal. Families have changed, as have the character of the relationships that they used to contain, and which, we should note, used to contain them.[40] However this change is not causal, it is part of the set of emergent conditions that have come to be appraised as late- or post-modernity.[41] It is within this context that, I argue, a new vision of childhood has arisen and one of the signposts towards this new vision is the unprecedented increase in child abuse from which this paper began. It is a vision very different from the 'futurity' of modernity.

Bell,[42] and later Touraine,[43] were perhaps the first to awaken our attention to the alteration in the traditional fabric of relations that made up modernity. Both these liberal, or indeed neo-Conservative, theorists revealed that traditional secular beliefs and taken-for-granted categories of community membership no longer prevailed. Bell, proclaiming an end to ideology, arguably instigated the era of the 'post-' with his thesis describing a change in both the mode and relations of production. The productive base, Bell and also Touraine informed us, had transmuted, through market forces and advances in technology, into the 'post-industrial', and the system of social stratification, long since recognizable in terms of polarization had, through a series of social movements, thickened at the waist to contain a middle-ing service class such as to diffuse conventional class antagonisms, thus becoming 'post-capitalist'. These two concepts, Bauman stated, 'have served the purpose well: they sharpened our attention to what is new and discontinuous, and offered us a reference point for counter arguments in favour of continuity'.[44]

Previously assumed points of attachment of the individual with the collective life, like social class, work group, local community and family, were now seen to be losing their adhesion in line with the demands of a post-Fordist mode of production, global economies and networks of communication, and the exponential inroads that techno-science continues to make into the previously located centres of knowledge and authority. Individuals are now much more recognizable through their immediate location and project than through their group affiliations or previously established identity. The new experience of history at both the individual level and the level of institutions, is one of discontinuity rather than of continuity.

The living through of modernity, a practice stemming from a firm belief in enlightenment and emancipation, gave rise to a confident cultural attitude of 'being in control'. This was a control based on: the possibility of objective knowledge through rational process; the primacy of centred, communicating selves; and the conviction that difference was reconcilable through analysis and discourse. Such bases ensured that the ensuing attitude was both sustaining and comfortable. This attitude was deeply rooted in the necessity, the viability, and the moral certainty of 'progress'. Human progress committed social action to the perpetual struggle for higher forms of life. Contingency, the condition that ruled the pre-modern (the 'savage' before Rousseau), was now part of a strategic calculus weighted in the favour of *homo sapiens* by the guarantees provided by our applied sciences.

The excitement and the purpose of social being, the dreams and the promise embedded in our children, was to reach for the stars, to control more and more of the wantonness of the cosmos, and to produce human culture as the triumph of finitude over infinity. What could not be achieved today could be set in train for tomorrow. The sufferings and deprivations and ignorance of our parents were certainly not going to be visited on the next generation, our future, our children. There would be no repeat of the Holocaust, but instead mass education and mass consumption. The ironies of this latter 'advancement' have not gone unnoticed:

> Consumerism pits the generations against one another. The all-knowing media child is the corporate terminal in families and schools without authority. Such children are accustomed to all the scarcities that derive from the outstripping of family income by family outgo, including their own part-time incomes. The result is that their own childhood is shortened, while its quality is thinned.[45]

But the striving to acquire, achieve and control sustains.

That the natural has become tamed, through modernity, ensures that all phenomena become both social and historical. In this sense the pre-modern contingency inverts and all phenomena become dependent upon human conduct, including their forms of knowledge and interpretive procedures. Despite the fact that nature occasionally strikes back, with a Los Angeles earthquake for example, its character is anticipated and its impact minimized. A new omnipotence was released into the human attitude, instancing perhaps a 'second passing' of the deity: the first recorded by Nietzschean irrationalism; the second etched onto the public memory by Hiroshima. However, as Heywood stated:

> This is not just to do with the problems attendant on the nature of modern weaponry and warfare, of global industrialization, of the revolutionary, 'deconstructive' impact of capitalist market systems on all aspects of human relationships. . . . At a deeper level it is related to the termination of nature and tradition in late-modernity.

And he continued that this has been expressed,

> in terms of the appearance of a fully socialized nature, marking the emergence of human power as globally decisive and unchallenged, without equal, limit, confining shape or *telos*, its old adversaries – nature and the 'second

nature' of traditional cultures now having been van-
quished. The possibility, indeed the necessity, of radical
self-formation confronts individuals, institutions and
whole societies. Opportunities to fulfil the emancipatory
promise of enlightenment are balanced by the potential
for social, ecological, political and cultural calamities on
an unprecedented scale.[46]

These observations are informed by Beck's[47] concept of a
'risk society', and they exemplify Giddens'[48] tightrope between
'ontological security' and 'existential anxiety'. Within these tendencies of late-modernity, personal actions and personal aspirations take on a different form. The previously centred,
continuous self of modernity becomes more of a reflexive project
involving disparate interactional planes rendered coherent
through a revisable narrative of self-identity. And, in the same
manner that institutions hold together through the ingenious
practice of 'crisis management', the reflexive project of the self
sustains through the artfully renewable strategies of auto/bio-
graphical stories. The late-modern calls forth a constant, reflexive,
re-presentation of self.[49] This is, of course, critical to the experience of being a child but more significantly, in the context of my
argument, critical in terms of how adults now understand and
relate to children.

The social spaces occupied by adults and children have
changed, not just in place but in character, and the spaces previously allocated to fixed identities of adults, and children, and
families have transmogrified. But this spatial dimension of social
experience is not alone in its new-found versatility, its pacing has
changed as well. Following a stable period of historical inevitability, we are now also witnessing innovations in the vocabulary
of time which drastically alter our relation to a whole set of
cultural configurations, established under modernity's motif of
'progress'. As Virilio has put it:

The loss of material space leads to the government of
nothing but time. . . . In this precarious fiction speed
would suddenly become a destiny, a form of progress, in
other words a 'civilization' in which each speed would be
something of a 'region' of time. . . . The violence of speed
has become both the location and the law, the world's
destiny and its destination.[50]

This impacts directly upon our vision of the child. Through modernity time itself was measured and contained, it came to be expressed in minutes, days, weeks, years and in categories such as generations. We marked out our personal ability, responsibility, functionality, mortality and general expectations of self, and others, through such divisions. We elected a periodic framework within which we might assemble unconnected events and ascribe to them the status of achievement or 'progress'. Generations have been gathered by such devices and the coincidental accumulation of social action has been defined under the detached title of a particular era[51] – like, for example, the 'swinging 60s'. Although the formal divisions on the clock and calendar are unchanged our collective expectations of appropriate chronological advancement have altered: people make late entry into education; marriage is not a necessary temporal goal and is also a repeatable experience; some families are established at the limit of a woman's band of fertility; some men become fathers at an age ensuring that they will not see their children through adolescence; occupational careers are interrupted and individuals opt for early retirement; vast numbers of people experience a lifetime of unemployment. The previously indelible normative markers of social experience (in the form of 'achievement' and 'status') are becoming relativized, sometimes through the pressure of material circumstances but equally because of the expression of a proliferation of new and different senses of 'purpose'. Indeed, 'purpose' is no longer linked to 'progress'. The higher forms of life, to which modernity since enlightenment aspired, were the utopias of freedom, equality, goodwill, peace and prosperity, all long recognized for their unattainability and their ideological content. Such utopias are now treated as mere ciphers, as hazy images deriving from the reveries of 'futurity', the dreams dreamt through children and through their childhood promise. When we return to real, active people, we witness not dreams, nor yet the realization of nightmares, but a pragmatic state of disenchantment. Rather than a life spent in pursuit of utopias the late-modern condition is one of the avoidance, or minimization, of dystopias. Horizontal strategies for the annulment of convention occur, a process of de-traditionalization. Alternative life-styles are so common and widespread as to find difficulty in expressing their alternativeness 'to'. For example, gross financial materialism lives alongside holistic medicine, health foods, body culture, astrology, narcotic addiction and dealing, arcane 'new age' belief systems, serial killers and single-parent families. This is no list of pathologies but a glimpse of the many facets of the late-modern experience, some are bizarre and criminal, others are benign or simply diverting. All of these expressions, and many others, are met in the street and all are now shadows of the mainstream.

In the context of this decline in collective aspiration, or 'disenchantment'[52] with the sense of purpose previously exercised by the concept of 'progress' (what Lyotard refers to as the death of a meta-narrative) people are resourceful in their search for both alternative reasons for being and also new points of attachment to a collective life. Although, as Giddens[53] argues, the late-modern individual may be less well imbued with a strong sense of the fixity of the inside and of cultural inheritance and may therefore have developed a robust adaptive strategy of bargaining and negotiation with the outside, it is nevertheless the case that members of a late-modern society continue to seek out both coherence of self-identity and continuity with the past.

It will be recalled that the classical sociological actors who populated Durkheim's emergent 'organic solidarity' at the end of the previous century, were perpetually insecure in the face of the potentially destructive 'anomic' forces inherent in modernity's form of the division of labour. Their external response was to develop a secular credo of interdependency, but their internal response was to re-establish a supportive mosaic of 'mechanical solidarities' in the form of work groups, professional guilds, churches and families. This inward search for coherence and continuity sustains into late-modernity but, as I have argued, these nineteenth-century sources of integration are not so readily available. However, there are two visible indices of the maintenance of an inward pilgrimage within late-modernity. The first, I suggest, is the obvious growth and, at the same time, destigmatization of psychotherapy in Western societies. Psychiatric and psychotherapeutic regimes tend to be conducted through regressive narratives with individuals 'finding their way' through the excavation of roots and attachments from the past – the 'inner child'. The second index is the real child, that is our new vision of the child and our practical relationship with it.

Late-modern society has re-adopted the child. The child in the setting of what are now conceptualized as post-modern cultural configurations, has become the site or the relocation of discourses concerning stability, integration and the social bond. The child is now envisioned as a form of 'nostalgia', a longing for times past, not as 'futurity'. Children are now seen not so much as 'promise' but as primary and unequivocal sources of love, but also as partners in the most fundamental, unchosen, unnegotiated form of relationship. The trust that was previously anticipated from marriage, partnership, friendship, class solidarity and so on, is now invested more generally in the child. This can be witnessed empirically in a number of ways: through the affectual prolongation of adolescence; the disputed territory that children constitute during parental divorce; the uprating of children's status through the modern advances in children's rights (like the 1989 Children Act in the UK); the modern iconography of the child in Third World aid politics and in Western campaigns against addiction and criminality.

The instability and necessary flexibility of all forms of relationship, other than that between adult and child, through late-modernity make them unreliable repositories for 'the inside', whether in the form of feelings, altruism or sociality itself. As Beck has stated:

> The child is the source of the last remaining, irrevocable, unexchangeable primary relationship. Partners come and go. The child stays. Everything that is desired, but not realizable in the relationship, is directed to the child. With the increasing fragility of the relationship between the sexes the child acquires a monopoly on practical companionship, on an expression of feelings in a biological give and take that otherwise is becoming increasingly uncommon and doubtful. Here an anachronistic social experience is celebrated and cultivated which has become improbable and longed for precisely because of the individualization process. The excessive affection for children, the 'staging of childhood' which is granted to them – the poor overloved creatures – and the nasty struggle for the children during and after divorce are some symptoms of this. The child becomes the final alternative to loneliness that can be built up against the vanishing possibilities of love. It is the private type of re-enchantment, which arises with, and derives its meaning from, disenchantment.[54]

Oddly enough, children are seen as dependable and permanent, in a manner to which no other person or persons can possibly aspire. The vortex created by the quickening of social change and the alteration of our perceptions of such change means that whereas children used to cling to us, through modernity, for guidance into their/our 'futures', now we, through late-modernity, cling to them for 'nostalgic' groundings, because such change is both intolerable and disorienting for us. They are lover, spouse, friend, workmate and, at a different level, symbolic representations of society itself. As Scutter stated in an analysis of children's literature:

> the child is characteristically associated with values that *seem* to be in opposition to those ascribed to adults, just as Peter Pan seems to be set in antithesis to the adult growing world. But the contemporary child and adolescent ... again and again proves to be a superior repository of those values the adult world ascribes to but falls short of. The child makes a better adult.[55]

Although this work is from within a literary textual world it is highly instructive. Peter Pan's Never Neverland is no longer a recalcitrant state from which children have to be prised to get on with 'futures'; it is, what was: love and care, reciprocity and sociality. Scutter continued: 'Neverland is actually not a child realm but an adult realm.'[56]

We need children as the sustainable, reliable, trustworthy, now outmoded treasury of social sentiments that they have come to represent. Our 'nostalgia' for their essence is part of a complex, late-modern, rearguard attempt at the resolution of the contradictory demands of the constant re-evaluation of value with the pronouncement of social identity.

As we need children we watch them and we develop institutions and programmes to watch them and oversee the maintenance of that which they, and they only, now protect. We have always watched children, once as guardians of their/our future and now because they have become the guardians. Our expanded surveillance has, needless to say, revealed more intrusions into their state of well-being. Child abuse, from which we began, has clearly 'increased' through the magnification and breadth of our gaze. This is evidenced from two sources.

First, as we noted earlier with reference to a shift in Kempe's perspective,[57] the 'invention' of child abuse in the 1960s seems to transform into a 'dis-covery' of child abuse in the 1970s. The prevalence of child abuse as a social practice, far from spontaneously regenerating in the second half of the twentieth century, had, in fact, been constant, which is testified to by Kempe's renewed interest in the historical dimension of the phenomenon. However, the incidence of child abuse during that period, in terms of reported and recorded occurrence, was to be treated as a novel phenomenon, an expanding phenomenon, and a phenomenon worthy of further explanation in itself; as I have attempted here.

The second source is Dingwall et al.[58] who, in making an essentially ethnomethodological point concerning the routine practices of rate-producing agencies, examine the psychological and social processes by which social workers decide whether or not children are being abused. Dingwall et al. develop the concept of professional strategies and put forward two models, the 'pessimistic' and the 'optimistic'. The former, it is suggested, is that which is adopted by social workers in the face of governmental, media, local and public pressure (for example, during the moral panic created by the 1987 Cleveland 'affair' in the UK) and consists of a 'better safe than sorry' approach, involving all children being regarded as potentially abused, which in turn leads to a dramatic increase in reported cases. The 'optimistic' strategy which derives from a different climate of expectation, or, ironically, emerges as a reaction to the backlash often caused by the former strategy, involves actual abuse being regarded, by social workers, as the least plausible diagnosis of a family problem.

Nevertheless, the dramatic increase in the reported occurrence of child abuse during late-modernity is not reducible solely to the improved technology of our scrutiny nor just to our diligence, however enforced. It is, as I have sought to argue, due to the intensity of the collective response to those very late-modern conditions. What is being so jealously preserved through the new, 'nostalgic', vision of the child is the meta-narrative of society itself. The story of the post-modern child and its abuse makes up a palimpsest.

To abuse the child today is to strike at the remaining, embodied vestige of the social bond and the consequent collective reaction is, understandably, both resounding and vituperative. The shrill cry of 'abuse' is a cry of our own collective pain at the loss of our social identity. The source of blame for this abuse whether projected into the form of psychopaths, perverts, devil-worshippers, colluding mothers, men, or even incompetent social workers should really be sought in the way that we have, over time, come to organize our social relationships.

CONCLUSION

With the acceleration of the pace of social change towards the end
of the twentieth century, the individual witnesses a diminution
of their points of attachment to a collective life, or at best
a recognition of the utterly transitory nature of such points
of attachment. With the dispersion, fragmentation and de-
traditionalization of established sources of judgement, such as the
cognitive, the ethical and the aesthetic, the individual experiences
increasing discontinuity between previously held interests, beliefs
and commitments and those of any coherent group. Politics
becomes mediated by speed and authority by risk. Where classical
sociology had pointed to the remedy for disintegration resting
with the establishment of an ethic of interdependency, no such
positive altruism or pragmatic reciprocity are now available
options. The current experience of subjectivity is a fierce tension
between dependency and independency.

> It was specifically in bourgeois society that an association
> between age and dependence was established. . . . Liber-
> ated from the necessity of labour yet excluded from the
> adult social world, childhood became an increasingly puz-
> zling phenomenon. Its sequestration was justified on the
> grounds of children's 'immaturity' and 'helplessness', on
> their evident need to be 'looked after'.[59]

However, dependency is no longer a taken-for-granted feature of
the relationship between adults and children, what with demands
for charters of children's rights, with children 'divorcing' from
parents, and the increasingly cynical backdrop of 'abuse', topical-
ized here, policing the exercise of all and any control between
adults and children. And it is certainly the case that dependency
is no longer a respectable feature of any relationship between
adults. Independence, it would seem, has become the dis-located
mark of personhood in the post-modern life, a criterion which
frees the self from the outmoded constraints of the old order but
precludes an analysis of the successful mechanisms of cultural
reproduction inherent within that structural order. As Coward
put it:

> We apply the term 'abuse' so widely that we are in danger
> of misrepresenting modern relations of social power. . . .
> Excessive concentration on abuse puts a question mark
> over dependency but does not allow us to understand or

criticise power. Instead it criticises character types – the abuser and the abused, the perpetrator and the victim – and pathologises their relationship. Abusers are now seen as the ultimate villains, more sinister than any who benefit from the real inequalities of society.[60]

Dependency rests on a need and an authority in the provision of that need – abuse requires the misuse or corruption of that authority. The post-modern diffusion of authority has not led to democracy but to an experience of powerlessness, this is not a potential source of identity but a prescription for victimization. Children, I am suggesting, figure largely as symbolic representations of this welter of uncertainty, both literally and metaphorically.

Political correctness, another post-modern regulator of experience, is a blanket strategy for the resistance to the imposition of any form of authority (primarily in linguistic form) and the current 'climate of abuse' derives from a sustained confusion between power and its legitimation.

Children have become both the testing ground for the necessity of independence in the constitution of human subjectivity and also the symbolic refuge of the desirability of trust, dependency and care in human relations. In this latter role 'childhood' sustains the 'meta-narrative' of society itself and abuse, both real and supposed, expresses our current ambivalence towards and impotence in the face of constantly emergent structural conditions. As we see less coherence and sustained meaning in the experience of our own subjectivity and our relationships with others, we witness more symbolic abuse of children.

We are compelled to care about the well-being and prospects of other people's children as a condition of preserving our nationhood. If the value placed on national life recedes, displaced by an ethos of autonomy and dissociation, our relations with children and each other change profoundly. Children lose their collective status, and are no longer the ancestral and progenitorial bond of national continuity. Instead, they become the private presences whose entry into the world is occasioned by the pursuit of private fulfilment. The child of choice becomes the responsibility of the adults who choose. The life quality and life chances of children increasingly reflect the arbitrary fortuities of family origin and genetic endowments.[61]

On what criteria could we possibly judge Medea today?

NOTES

[1] See P. Bourdieu, 'Systems of education and systems of thought' in M. Young (ed.), *Knowledge and Control*, London: Collier-Macmillan, 1971; C. Jenks (ed.), *Cultural Reproduction*, London: Routledge, 1993; J. Donald, *Sentimental Education*, London: Verso, 1992.

[2] P. Ariès, *Centuries of Childhood*, London: Cape, 1962; L. DeMause (ed.), *The History of Childhood*, London: Souvenir, 1976; L. Stone, *The Family, Sex and Marriage in England, 1500–1800*, London: Weidenfeld & Nicolson, 1977; L. Pollock, *Forgotten Children: Parent-Child Relations from 1500 to 1900*, Cambridge: Cambridge University Press, 1983; J. Demos, *Past, Present and Personal*, Oxford: Oxford University Press, 1986; R. Houlbrooke, *The English Family 1450–1700*, London: Longman, 1984; J. Boswell, *The Kindness of Strangers: The Abandonment of Children in Western Europe from Late Antiquity to the Renaissance*, Harmondsworth: Penguin, 1988.

[3] J. Sommerville, *The Rise and Fall of Childhood*, Beverly Hills, CA: Sage, 1982.

[4] C. Kempe, F. Silverman, B. Steele, W. Droegemueller and H. Silver, 'The battered child syndrome' in *Journal of the American Medical Association*, no. 181, 1962, pp. 17–24.

[5] D. Finkelhor, *Sexually Victimized Children*, New York: Free Press, 1979.

[6] J. Garbarino and G. Gilliam, *Understanding Abusive Families*, Cambridge, MA: Lexington Books, 1980.

[7] N. Caplan and S. Nelson, 'On being useful: the nature and consequences of psychological research into social problems' in *American Psychologist*, vol. 28, 1973, pp. 199–211.

[8] D. Finkelhor, *Child Sexual Abuse: New Theory and Research*, New York: Free Press, 1984, p. 3.

[9] R. Dingwall, J. Eekelaar and T. Murray, *The Protection of Children: State Intervention and Family Life*, Oxford: Blackwell, 1986.

[10] P. Stallybrass and A. White, *The Politics and Poetics of Transgression*, London: Methuen, 1986.

[11] E. Jones, *Sigmund Freud: Life and Work*, vol. 2, London: Hogarth Press, 1955, pp. 13–14.

[12] W. Stainton Rogers, D. Hevey and E. Ash (eds), *Child Abuse and Neglect – Facing the Challenge*, London: Open University, 1989.

[13] G. Mayes, E. Currie, L. Macleod, J. Gilles and D. Warden, *Child Sexual Abuse*, Edinburgh: Scottish Academic Press, 1992.

[14] H. Ferguson, *The Science of Pleasure*, London: Routledge, 1990, p. 11.

[15] D. Finkelhor, 1984, op. cit.

[16] P. Abbott, 'Family lifestyles and structures' in W. Stainton Rogers *et al.* (eds), op. cit.

[17] V. DeFrancis, *Protecting the Victim of Sex Crimes Committed by Adults*, Denver: American Humane Association, 1969; D. Finkelhor, 1979, op. cit.; D. Finkelhor, 1984, op. cit.; R. Summit and J. Kryso, 'Sexual abuse of children: A clinical spectrum' in *American Journal of Orthopsychiatry*, vol. 48, no. 2, 1978, pp. 237–251; D. Russell, 'The incidence and prevalence of intrafamilial and extrafamilial sexual abuse of female children' in *Child Abuse and Neglect*, no. 7, 1983, pp. 133–146; J. Herman, *Father–Daughter Incest*, Cambridge, MA: Harvard University Press, 1981; J. Haugaard and N. Reppucci, *The Sexual Abuse of Children: A Comprehensive Guide to Current Knowledge and Intervention Strategies*, London: Jossey-Bass, 1988.

[18] G. Gelles and C. Cornell, *Intimate Violence in Families*, Beverly Hills: Sage, 1985.

[19] R. Inglis, *Sins of the Fathers*, London: Peter Owen, 1978; M. Jobling, 'Child abuse: the historical and social context' in V. Carver (ed.), *Child Abuse: A Study Text*, Milton Keynes: Open University, 1978; R. Kempe and C. Kempe, *Child Abuse*, London: Fontana, 1978.

[20] M. Freeman, *Violence in the Home: A Socio-Legal Study*, Farnborough: Gower, 1979.

[21] R. Kempe and C. Kempe, op. cit., p. 17.

[22] C. Kempe and R. Helfer, *The Battered Child*, London: University of Chicago Press, 1980.

[23] M. Foucault, *Politics, Philosophy, Culture*, L. Kritzman (ed.), New York: Routledge, 1988, p. 302.

[24] G. Mayes *et al.*, op. cit.
[25] M. DeYoung, *The Sexual Victimization of Children*, Jefferson, NC: McFarland, 1982; R. Brant and V. Tisza, 'The sexually misused child' in *American Journal of Orthopsychiatry*, vol. 47, no. 1, 1977, pp. 80–90.
[26] J. Herman and L. Hirschman, 'Father–daughter incest', *Signs* 2, 1977, pp. 1–22; F. Rush, *The Best Kept Secret: Sexual Abuse of Children*, New York: McGraw-Hill, 1980; S. Nelson, *Incest – Fact and Myth*, Strathmullion Co-operative Ltd, 1982; E. Ward, *Father–Daughter Rape*, London: Women's Press, 1984.
[27] S. Brownmiller, *Against Our Will: Men, Women and Rape*, New York: Simon & Schuster, 1975.
[28] V. Bell, *Interrogating Incest: Feminism, Foucault and the Law*, London: Routledge, 1993, p. 3.
[29] B. Corby, *Child Abuse: Towards a Knowledge Base*, Buckingham: Open University Press, 1993.
[30] Ibid., p. 16.
[31] R. Williams, *The Long Revolution*, Harmondsworth: Penguin, 1965.
[32] U. Bronfenbrenner, *Two Worlds of Childhood*, Harmondsworth: Penguin, 1974, p. 1.
[33] C. Jenks, *The Sociology of Childhood: Essential Readings*, London: Batsford, 1982; J. O'Neill, 'Embodiment and child development: a phenomenological approach' in H. Dreitzel (ed.), *Recent Sociology No. 5*, New York: Macmillan, 1973.
[34] J. Donzelot, *The Policing of Families*, London: Hutchinson, 1986.
[35] D. Cooper, *The Death of the Family*, Harmondsworth: Penguin, 1972.
[36] W. Stainton Rogers *et al.*, op. cit., 1989, p. 10.
[37] L. DeMause, op. cit.
[38] P. Ariès, op. cit.
[39] J. Boswell, op. cit.
[40] J. Wallerstein and S. Blakeslee, *Second Chances*, London: Bantam, 1989; A. Giddens, *Modernity and Self-Identity*, Cambridge: Polity Press, 1991; U. Beck, *Risk Society: Towards a New Modernity*, London: Sage, 1992; J. Stacey, *Brave New Families*, New York: Basic Books, 1990; C. Lasch, *The Culture of Narcissism*, London: Abacus, 1980.
[41] J. Lyotard, *The Postmodern Condition: A Report on Knowledge*, Manchester: Manchester University Press, 1986; Z.

Bauman, *Intimations of Postmodernity*, London: Routledge, 1992; B. Smart, *Postmodernity*, London: Routledge, 1993.

[42] D. Bell, *The Coming of Post-Industrial Society: A Venture in Social Forecasting*, New York: Basic Books, 1973.

[43] A. Touraine, 'Is sociology still the study of society?' in *Thesis Eleven*, no. 23, 1989; A. Touraine, 'The waning sociological image of social life' in *International Journal of Comparative Sociology*, vol. 25, nos 1 & 2, 1984.

[44] Z. Bauman, 'Is there a postmodern sociology?' in *Theory, Culture and Society*, vol. 5, nos 2–3, 1988, p. 217.

[45] J. O'Neill, *The Missing Child in Liberal Theory*, Toronto: University of Toronto Press, 1994, p. 106.

[46] I. Heywood, 'An art of scholars: negation and particularity in paintings by Ryman and Richter' in C. Jenks (ed.), *Visual Culture*, London: Routledge, 1995, pp. 128–129.

[47] U. Beck, op. cit.

[48] A. Giddens, op. cit.

[49] E. Goffman, *Relations in Public*, London: Allen Lane, 1971.

[50] P. Virilio, *Speed and Politics*, New York: Semiotext(e), 1986, pp. 141, 151.

[51] D. Chaney, *The Cultural Turn*, London: Routledge, 1994.

[52] U. Beck, op. cit.

[53] A. Giddens, op. cit.

[54] U. Beck, op. cit., p. 118.

[55] H. Scutter, 'Representing the child: postmodern versions of Peter Pan', paper presented at Issues in Australian Childhood conference, QUT, Brisbane, 1993, p. 12.

[56] Ibid., p. 12.

[57] R. Kempe and C. Kempe, op. cit.

[58] R. Dingwall *et al.*, op. cit.

[59] H. Ferguson, op. cit., p. 11.

[60] R. Coward, 'Culture obsessed with abuse' in the *Observer*, 6 June 1993.

[61] M. Novick, 'Foreword' to J. O'Neill, *The Missing Child in Liberal Theory*, Toronto: University of Toronto Press, 1994, p. vii.

5

The strange death of childhood[1]

> Children are the living messages we send to a time we will not see. From a biological point of view it is inconceivable that any culture will forget that it needs to reproduce itself. But it is quite possible for a culture to exist without children. Unlike infancy, childhood is a social artifact, not a biological category.[2]

Such is the character of Postman's opening remarks when he sets his thesis concerning the 'disappearance of childhood'. Birth is a necessity but what follows is entirely a matter of historical contingency. The work contains an apocalyptic vision concerning the end of childhood as we know it and a necessary collapse of the social category that it inhabits. All now is the province of the adult consciousness and, Postman is suggesting, at what loss? Thus we reveal the real topic which is the challenge to and subsequent corrosion of the human condition through the penetration of global techno-science into the lifeworld of all in the late twentieth century. Children are then the first casualties of the articulation of culture through mass media.

Postman argues that childhood has a relatively recent history and was essentially brought into being through the era of mass literacy and mass education. It was at this critical historical moment that the new medium of print brought about and imposed a categorical distinction between child and adult. The written word both fixed and politicized the difference as the cultural amnesia of oral traditions gave way to objective record, and previously supposed social homogeneity gave way to the necessary recognition of heterogeneity. However, as Postman informs us, the contemporary media of late-modernity exercise a different function and serve to disassemble established taxonomies. Postman explores the new media through his concept of *technopoly*, a kind of cultural hegemony of images and image production, which he sees in the form of film and, primarily, television but which more recent work has examined in terms of computer pornography[3] and surfing the internet. These new forms of media are now systematically undermining that distinction between child and adult due to an indifference to difference generated through economies in production or the drive to create new and uniform categories of consumer. As a consequence, childhood is disappearing. A child, subject to a diet of violence, sexuality, exploitation and a persistent invitation to consume cannot sustain an autonomous realm of being. Thus the new media conveys and creates the message that childhood is no more.

> The evidence for the disappearance of childhood comes in several varieties and from different sources. There is, for example, the evidence displayed by the media themselves, for they not only promote the unseating of childhood through their form and context but reflect its decline in their content. There is evidence to be seen in the merging of the taste and style of children and adults, as well as in the changing perspectives of relevant social institutions such as the law, the schools, and sports. And there is evidence of the 'hard' variety – figures about alcoholism, drug use, sexual activity, crime etc., that imply a fading distinction between childhood and adulthood.[4]

Postman's views are not without critics[5] and it would be incorrect to assume that the argument I am about to produce is supportive of the 'disappearance' thesis. What support it does claim is often in the guise of right-wing political rhetoric and moral backlash opinion concerning the collapse of the family, or rather berating emergent modes of parenting, and predicting a future society stratified according to the socialization experience of its members. However, we do need to attend to a tacit acceptance of a gathering sense of loss of or at least a blurring of the category of childhood that is implicit in more serious debates about the interests and rights of children, the public or private responsibility for children, the dependence or independence of children, and the empowerment, enfranchisement, economic autonomy and criminalization of children. It is with this last point that I begin.

In many senses we might suggest that the innocence of childhood has finally come of age. The lyrical image of childhood as the 'sleep of reason', initiated by Rousseau, was subsequently amplified by Goya into the more sinister version that 'the sleep of reason produces monsters!' In 1993 in the UK, this was a prophecy which, at last, seemed to have come true through the brutal murder of one child by two others.

> James Bulger was a month short of his third birthday when two killers lured him away from his mother in a busy shopping mall, dragged him to a lonely railway embankment and murdered him. It was an unspeakably cruel death. The thought of anyone being cruel enough to inflict such a fate on an innocent little child defies comprehension. Astonishingly, the killers in this case were both just ten years old.[6]

Not yet diminished by the passage of time nor by the imposition of guilty verdicts on two young boys and the Home Secretary Michael Howard's subsequent retributive recommendation of a fifteen-year minimum period of containment for them both, a feeling of terrible uncertainty and public unease remains more than a year after this 'shocking' event. My concern here is to tease out the nature and import of that unease.

I start out from the suggestion that the murder was not just disturbing, but was, quite literally, inconceivable. Inconceivable, that is, because it occurred within the conceptual space of childhood which, prior to this breach, was thought of – for the most part and for most children – as innocence enshrined. In essence, what the British public seemed to have to come to terms with in 1993 was that childhood could no longer be envisioned unproblematically as a once-upon-a-time story with a happy and predictable ending.

However, in vaunting the apparent originality of this transgression of our childhood categories, we should not be forgetful of the spectacular precedent provided by the double child-murder committed by the twelve-year-old Mary Bell in the UK in 1968,[7] nor the largely unwritten history of child-by-child murders that undoubtedly preceded it. What was remarkable in the context of the 1993 incident, however, was an apparent dense public forgetfulness about these earlier events. Little evidenced in the highly voluble and condemnatory public concern about children and violence which took place in the press, this amnesia sheds some light, albeit refracted, on the divergent understandings of childhood which were expressed at that time.

As anguish vied with outrage, calls for retribution and revenge were at least matched by those for compassion and understanding and a demand for the increasing secular policing of children was championed in the context of a tardy response by the church to condemn. Indicative of an ambivalence abroad in the wider population, the rapid yet unconsidered reaction of some sections of the laity simply served to emphasize the apparent reluctance of the clergy to engage in such a high profile moral issue, seemingly providing further evidence, in addition to the murder, of a nation in a state of moral decline.

> Childcare experts say the idea that children can be inherently evil has gained currency since the Bulger trial. Roger Smith, social policy officer for the Children's Society, said: 'The trial was held at a time when there was serious concern about joy-riding and other juvenile crime. There was a feeling that it was all getting out of control. It was easier to put it down to children's "evil" nature rather than confront the complexity of the problem.'
>
> The Government seemed keen to catch the public mood. The Home Secretary promised 'tough action' on juvenile crime and, Mr. Smith believes, is introducing inappropriate measures to deal with delinquent children, including a plan to put more 12- to 14-year-old offenders in secure units. The 'evil child' lobby took heart from recent – inaccurate – reports from the United States claiming that a 'criminal gene' had been identified.[8]

None the less, these varied responses shared common themes, themes which questioned the idea of 'the child' and the institution of childhood in the late twentieth century. They centred on two interlinked issues: first, what is 'the child's' nature and second, what are the limits of 'the child's' capacity for action? That these are neither original nor unusual questions about childhood is itself pertinent to my concerns, for they underline the socially constructed nature of childhood, a childhood with which children themselves have to engage daily.[9]

We should begin then with an examination of the conceptual framework that has provided for the continued dominance of the image of childhood innocence in British culture. In addition we need to seek to understand the public responses to the murder of Jamie Bulger. Here I shall address a particular range of public responses, namely certain opinions expressed through the pages of the quality press. And I shall attempt to highlight, from the perspective of sociology, the issues it raised about the place of children in contemporary British society through its seeming negation of that dominant image of innocence. However, as in all of the chapters in this book, our topic is childhood. This is neither an essay about criminology nor the media *per se*. My consideration of media representations is, therefore, purposefully restricted to a limited range of articles and commentaries available from the quality press. Such a methodology does not seek to achieve a representative sample but rather the reverse; that is, it demonstrates that even within this one narrow branch of the media a surprisingly wide spectrum of responses were available thus providing further evidence of the radical disruption which children who commit violent crime apparently bring to our concepts of 'the child'.

A further point of this chapter is to indicate what this debate portends for actual children through exploring the questions it prompted about the ideological construction, and therefore purpose, of 'childhood' itself.

To begin, however, we should note some dramatic and powerful consequences of this rupturing of our culturally and historically specific vision of childhood: not only has the Bulger murder given rise to a broad public debate about the nature of childhood, albeit often ill-informed, it may have also depotentiated the ideological role which 'childhood' has traditionally played in public perceptions of children and social relations more generally. Beyond this lies the potential consequences of such a changed perception of 'childhood' for children themselves which, as yet, remain to be fully spelled out.

TRADITIONAL CONCEPTIONS OF CHILDHOOD?

That there is a particular vision of Western childhood which is both historically and culturally specific is now well-established. The French historian Ariès,[10] whom we have already encountered, was one of the first to demonstrate that while children are present in all cultures their presence has been and still is differently regarded.[11] The biological facts of infancy are but the raw material upon which cultures work to fashion a particular version of 'being a child'. Thus, to have been a child in seventeenth-century England was, so the argument goes, a very different social experience from being a twentieth-century child, not only in terms of the material conditions of their existence but, more importantly, in relation to the duties, obligations, restraints and expectations placed upon children. In brief, what a child is reflects the particularities of particular socio-cultural contexts. This canon has been augmented by Sennet when he stated that:

> Ariès . . . opened up a whole new field – the study of the family as a historical form, rather than as a fixed biological form in history. Ariès found . . . that by the middle of the 18th Century adults were beginning to think about themselves as fundamentally different kinds of creatures from those who were their children. The child was no longer thought of as a little adult. Childhood was conceived as a special and vulnerable stage; adulthood was defined in reverse terms. The evidence Ariès uses is mostly from the family records of urban people in the middle and upper reaches of society. There is a reason for this; this same articulation of life stages served these people in defining the limits of public life. What was occurring in the cosmopolitan centres was that the mature people who inhabited them began to think of the public life, with all its complexities, its poses, and, above all, the routine encounters with strangers, as a life which only adults were strong enough to withstand and enjoy.[12]

More recently, however, a growing number of sociologists and anthropologists have attended to the dissonance which exists between children's own experiences of being a child and the institutional form which childhood takes.[13] This has sharpened a theoretical focus on the plurality of childhoods, a plurality evidenced not only cross-culturally but also within cultures. At the very least, it is suggested, the experience of childhood is fragmented and stratified, by class, age, gender and ethnicity, by urban or rural locations and by particularized identities cast for children through disability or ill health.

But, despite these different social experiences, children themselves remain enmeshed in the forced commonality of an ideological discourse of childhood. Routinely, children find their daily lives shaped by statutes regulating the pacing and placing of their experience. Compulsory schooling, for example, restricts their access to social space and gerontocratic prohibitions limit their political involvement, sexual activity, entertainment and consumption. Children are further constrained not only by implicit socializing rules which work to set controls on behaviour and limits on the expression of unique intent, but also by customary practices which, through the institution of childhood, articulate the rights and duties associated with 'being a child'.

For Western children these are still largely the rights and duties of the innocent abroad. Constrained by dominant paediatric and psychological theories of child development,[14] contemporary childhood remains an essentially protectionist experience. Obliged by the adult world to be happy, children, Ennew argues, are seen 'as lacking responsibility, having rights to protection and training but not to autonomy'.[15] Although derived from a particular spatio-temporal location, these ideal behavioural traits have been identified, none the less, as pertinent for all children. And simultaneous images of otherness are produced: those parents who fail to promulgate or accommodate this vision of childhood within the family are effectively seen to fail as parents and those children who fail to conform to the image of 'the child' are seen as some of childhood's failures.[16]

Testimony to the insidious and assiduous power of this particular discourse on childhood is found in the extensive globalization of Western ideas of childhood. As a post-colonial legacy, variation in the form which childhood might take is denied[17] as, through the Declaration of the Rights of the Child and the work of charitable agencies and international bodies in the Third World, one particular vision of childhood has been and continues to be exported as 'correct childhood'.[18] Not only does this cast doubt, and comparative judgement, upon different family forms and parenting practices in the Third World through the misguided, and tacit, assumption of a uniformity of childhood in

Western Europe, it also disguises the complex socially constructed character of 'the child' upon which it rests.[19]

But what, then, are the supposed intrinsic characteristics of 'the child' from which such a dominant idea of childhood springs? In their historical account of the emergence of contemporary ideas of childhood, Hockey and James[20] note four contributory themes which, during the last three centuries, have shaped a particular vision of what childhood is: (i) that the child is set apart temporally as different, through the calculation of age; (ii) that the child is deemed to have a special nature, determined by Nature; (iii) that the child is innocent; and (iv) therefore is vulnerably dependent. In sum, these are themes which centre, first, on questions of the child's morality (ii and iii); and second, on its capability (i and iv). And, as we have already suggested, it is precisely these themes which surfaced in the recent public debates about children and violent crime. Thus, the extent to which the shocking events of 1993 marked a significant shift in our understanding of childhood, rather than simply representing an old debate in a new guise is a central question for this chapter.

THE MORAL GROUND?

From a sociological perspective the issues raised by children who commit violent crime are first, conceptual, and second, empirical. But the two are intimately linked, for it is clear that the way in which we think about children and conceive of childhood has very practical consequences for children themselves. If, as I have argued throughout this book, childhood is a social construction which provides both form and content to children's experiences, then the ways in which children relate and are related to in everyday life is, inevitably, in terms of the conceptual structures through which they are previously envisaged. In brief, children are locked, for their intelligibility, within the contingency of social conventions. The negotiable character of these conventions is a question of power, which children can only exercise in a partial form. They can demand attention but not redefinition. How then is 'the child' defined and what might be the child's response?

An archaeology of the ideas which give rise to the modern 'child' reveals a strong and continuous commitment to conceptions of childhood innocence. First, emanating from Rousseau, children are awarded a purity, by virtue of their special nature. Emerging from the Enlightenment, they are the Ideal immanence, and the messengers of Reason. It is the experience of society which corrupts them. Left to its own devices the child would by nature, it was supposed, be guiltless. A second engagement with childhood innocence stems from Locke: children are thought to be innocent, not innately, but, like halfwits, as a consequence of their lack of social experience. Through time the unknowing, unworldly child may become corrupted by society.

Although formulated in the eighteenth century these perceptions of the child's moral nature and development have retained a powerful and persuasive hold upon the public imagination, reappearing in different guises and with different consequences for children themselves. For example, Freud's discussion of childhood sexuality[21] led to a contemporary furore and two decades of abuse for reinvoking 'original sin' in a libidinal form. Similarly, the contesting voices of nineteenth-century social reformers, discussed by Hendrick,[22] reveal, by turns, a concern to rescue the vulnerable child forced into factories and productive work and a desire to restore the Romantic innocence of childhood for all children, perceived to be under threat from working-class juvenile delinquency. So also, Kitzinger[23] shows how the untainted character of childhood has more recently been mobilized in a variety of forms in discussions about child sexual abuse, arguing that, for children themselves, such imagery is double-edged.

Notwithstanding differences in accounts of childhood's state of being, nor yet of the purpose and intent of its usage over time, the theme of innocence has remained closely tied to 'the child'. It would be hard to envisage any other group in modern society content to be suspended within such essentially anachronistic visions.

Nevertheless they persist. Charity adverts for overseas development and aid, for example, manipulate images of children's compliant part in their own deprivation,[24] emphasizing that children are the least complicit in causality yet the most affected. Similarly, it is as a passive victim of abuse, neglect and poverty that 'the child' is often displayed for the British public through mass media and Government rhetoric. In sum, a dominant modern discourse of childhood continues to mark out 'the child' as innately innocent, confirming its cultural identity as a passive and unknowing dependent, and therefore as a member of a social group utterly disempowered – but for good, altruistic reasons.

The view of children as being in possession of a special and distinctive nature, which is both innocent and vulnerably dependent, is what makes any link between children and violent crime particularly problematic, for the imagery of childhood and that of violent criminality are iconologically irreconcilable. It is still difficult, for example, to regard the video films of Jamie Bulger's abduction from the shopping mall as anything other than pictures of children holding hands. For the same reasons, it is impossible to ascribe blame to the apparent inaction of the many adults who witnessed the subsequent dismal procession to the fateful railway embankment. The transgressive juxtaposition of mundanity and magnitude in the freeze-frame footage of Jamie's abduction has been well stated by Sheila Johnston:

> The moment when James Bulger was led off to his death is known to us with uncommon precision: 12 February 1993, at 15 hours, 42 minutes and 32 seconds: the time-code on the surveillance camera which snatched a glimpse of the child leaving the crowded shopping centre at Bootle, Merseyside. Reproduced on posters, then on television later that month, resurrected again at the trial of James's tormentors, the blurred video footage had something about it that took the country by the throat.
>
> Was it the toddler himself, trotting along so trustingly, hand-in-hand with an elder boy? The cruel irony which had a Mothercare store sign presiding over the image?[25]

That these images were not of sweet, decent and honest children but of children perpetrating a violent and seemingly premeditated crime has had two important and highly disruptive consequences. First, the traditional image of 'the child' has been shattered through the dramatic denial of childish innocence. Second, the unitary idea of 'the child', which such an ideology so long encouraged, has been revealed as illusory. No longer confined to the academy, the idea that childhood is contestable and culturally variable has entered a more public arena. No longer can 'different' children be othered from the category of 'child'.

However, as stated at the outset of this chapter, it does not follow from this argument here that we should regard the recent conflation of the categories of 'child' and 'murderer' as instancing a unique state of affairs. Just as it has been established[26] that although child-abuse has only been rendered visible as a phenomenon during the last thirty years, its rate of historical occurrence has been virtually constant, so, we might suppose that children did not kill children for the first time either in the case of Mary

Bell or in Merseyside in 1993. We must assume and acknowledge that some children have always killed other children. What should concern us more here, from a sociological perspective, is the social context, the climate of collective sentiment which made this particular event utterly 'shocking' and disruptive in its consequences. Child-by-child murder may not constitute a social trend, nor is it an original event, but the magnitude of the public reaction to the Bulger case certainly does comprise a social phenomenon. Our concern here should not be to account for the death of a child, but to attempt to explain the imminent, and historically located, strange death of 'childhood' which, in 1993, became a pressing public concern.

Two main but contradictory themes dominated the developing debate about childhood begun in the autumn of 1993. First, that children can and do commit acts of violence voiced the possibility that, after all, the Puritans were correct; that children are born sinful and have a natural propensity for evil unless properly and rigorously restrained. This doctrine of Adamic 'original sin' is a model of childhood that I have previously formulated as the 'Dionysian' and have described as an image of wilful and unconstrained potential which has always provided the dark side or inarticulate backdrop to our contemporary and dominant images of innocence. As noted earlier, for instance, it was awakened this century in the powerful form of Freud's id and, more contemporarily, in debates about child sexual abuse.

A second, more liberal, interpretative framework, suggested that children who kill are simply anomalous. Such children, it was said, are literally out of step with the staged intellectual, social and moral development of 'normal' children. They were not, however, to be subsequently regarded as the falsifying 'black swans' of Popper's philosophy of science, but rather as the abhorrent cases in a search for the security, and dubious consensus, of the confirmation of childhood innocence.

To foreshadow some conclusions: the consequences of either the 'origin sin' or the 'anomalous case' responses is a re-construction, rather than radical re-think, of our attitudes to children through shifting and strengthening the existing conceptual boundaries of childhood so as to exclude, as pathological or peculiar, those children who exceed the limits of what it is to be a child. For children themselves this raises the possibility of an increased governing[27] of their activities through calls for visible forms of containment or, perhaps more implicit and possibly more repressive, calls for the reaffirmation of a concept of 'the normal child'. Such a response addresses not the moral grounds of the problem but rather defers this question through the modern recourse to further surveillance in the place of understanding. The dark spectre of Foucault's watchtower is brought to mind again along with the mechanical reduction of human conduct wrought through the one-sided emphasis on the 'voir' in 'savoir'.[28]

In November 1993 the rough framework of these debates began to be sketched in as, seemingly, society struggled to comprehend a growing disillusionment with what children are or might become in the modern world. It was not just two children who were on trial for the murder of a third but childhood itself. The death of Jamie Bulger became, in the broadest sense, a metaphor for the supposed moral decline of a society which experiences the exponential acceleration of social change[29] in late-modernity as the constant confrontation with the unfamiliar, that is, with 'risk'.[30] But such a sense of decline, as the assumed 'disappearance of childhood', should be tempered along with our, now routine, experience of risk. Note Douglas in this context:

> The very word 'risk' could well be dropped from politics.
> 'Danger' would do the work it does just as well. When
> 'risk' enters as a concept in political debate, it becomes
> a menacing thing, like a flood, an earthquake, or a thrown
> brick. But it is not a thing, it is a way of thinking, and a
> highly artificial contrivance at that.[31]

WHAT IS 'THE CHILD'?

That children are capable of violence, of rape, muggings and even murder, is an idea that clearly falls outside traditional formulations of childhood. As people privately struggled to make sense of the events of 1993, newspaper headlines echoed their confusion, a confusion engendered by children revealed in a new role as suspects in a hitherto adult crime:

> 'It is supposed to be the age of innocence so how could
> these 10 year olds turn into killers?'
>
> (*The Sunday Times*, 28 November 1993)

The problem voiced here is one of classification: children who commit such violent acts pose a conundrum for they disassemble the traditional binary opposition between the categories of 'child' and 'adult', an opposition previously legitimized by the peculiar gloss of the moral ground, outlined above, whereby innocence is a hallmark of 'the child' and corrupting knowledge that of the 'adult'. These categories became badly blurred as the literally unthinkable was transformed by a grim reality. The conceptual boundaries once containing the child, through 'is' or 'ought', became utterly indefensible. Public attempts at propitiation in the face of this potentially dangerous confusion were conducted in different ways.

One approach was through conceptual eviction: children who commit acts of violence should be removed from the category of 'child' altogether. Such expulsion facilitates the restoration of the old moral order and re-establishes the discourse of childhood in its traditional ideological form. Such strategies were apparent in press commentaries and readers' letters during November 1993 where images of radical alterity were routinely employed:

> 'evil freaks'
>> (*The Sunday Times*, 28 November 1993)

with

> '. . . the Satan Bug inside'
>> (*The Sunday Times*, 28 November 1993)

and having:

> '. . . adult brains'
>> (*The Sunday Times*, 28 November 1993)

as

> '. . . the spawn of Satan [who committed] . . . acts of unparalleled evil and barbarity.'
>> (*Guardian*, 27 November 1993)

These

> '. . . little devils'
>> (*The Sunday Times*, 28 November 1993)

were no longer to be classified as children.

Within these quotations two kinds of 'Otherness' can be identified: (a) the child possessed of an inherently evil nature; and (b) the composite creature, the 'adult-child'. Both are highly transgressive images, at once wilful, bizarre and demonic. In that these images instance acute fractures from the commonplace idea of 'the child' as it is understood within Western society, they both constitute a powerful and volatile ambiguity in public accounts of childhood. Anthropological work on social classification enables us to understand such a response as one emitting from a people whose cosmologies are under threat. As Douglas[32] has shown, the identification of anomalies, whether in the form of people, plants or animals, is integral to the establishment of social order: 'A polluting person is always in the wrong. He has developed some wrong condition or simply crossed some line which should not have been crossed and this displacement unleashes danger for someone.'[33]

Anomalies are, in essence, the by-products of systems of ordering. Through their remarked differences, ironically, they work to firm up the boundaries which give form and substance to the conceptual categories from which they are excluded:

> The idea of society is a powerful image. It is potent in its own right to control or to stir men to action. This image has form; it has external boundaries, margins, internal structure. Its outlines contain power to reward conformity and repulse attack. There is an energy in its margins and unstructured areas. For symbols of society any human experience of structures, margins or boundaries is ready to hand.[34]

In this sense, by refusing children who commit acts of violence acceptance within the category of child, the public was reaffirming to itself the essence of what children are (and thereby also reaffirming its commitment to a 'shared' social order). That is, it was a way to restore the primary image of the innate innocence of children through relegating some would-be children (those who commit acts of violence) to another category essentialized through images of evil or pathology. Thus, the stigma of anomaly works to explain how certain children are capable of actions which other, 'normal', children are not: the system of classification stays intact by resisting the 'defilement' of the abhorrent case.

That the kinds of responses, previously reported, were to be found in the pages of the quality press (and were not just tabloid rhetoric) indicates the powerful magnetism which the idea of 'the child' exercises in our thinking about the quality of our culture, its past achievements and the future collective moral 'good'. The child has become emblematic.

Other extracts from contemporaneous press reports suggest

that eroding the idea of 'the child' in late-modernity portends an even greater social loss: the loss of society itself. Thus, alongside the positing of innate evil and depravity as ways of accounting for why children commit violent crimes, other accounts struggled to explore the particularity of the social contexts, like dysfunctional families, which might foster, in the child, the ability to perform adult-like actions. As such they were attempting to salvage the idea of the child, by regarding it as an epiphenomenon.

Although seeming to represent an oppositional voice, this latter perspective shares a common ground: it too individualizes acts of violence in an attempt to cling onto traditional accounts of what children are. As an explanatory narrative it has as its source the fact that, as I argued in the previous chapter, 'the child' has become a way of speaking about sociality itself. Any assault on what the child is, or rather, what the child has evolved into, threatens to rock the social base. The child through the passage of modernity came to symbolize tomorrow and was thus guarded and invested. In the late-modern context, where belief in progress and futures has diminished, has the child come now to symbolize the solidity and adhesion of the past? And is it therefore defended as a hedge against an anxiety[35] wrought through the disappearance of the social bond rather than the disappearance of the child?

The divergent spectrum of public attitudes towards childhood criminality featured in the press and sublimated these contradictions. For those who would adhere to the view that evil is a genuine motivational force within the social world, the fact that children can commit acts of violence was simply an indication of how far we, as a society, had fallen from grace. Perhaps it even provided the spur for a 'return to basics' campaign. However, for those others adopting a more liberal stance, childhood criminality was regarded as a harbinger of how our nemesis would appear if we did not act to arrest the post-modern malaise.

A reader's letter published in the *Guardian* exemplifies one end of the spectrum of attitudes, that of the child-as-society:

'I was not surprised by the murder of James Bulger. It seemed to me just the sort of thing that could happen in nineties Britain, just one symptom of the insidious brutalism that has permeated every aspect of life. Why should we expect children to have any sense of mutuality when they grow up in a society where human life is accorded no value.'

(Guardian, 27 November 1993)

The opposite end appears in an adjacent letter:

'As children are treated, so they treat others. Each time a child is struck, it dies a little inside. Each time a society refuses to deal with causes of violence, it dies a little too.'

(Guardian, 27 November 1993)

And the two accounts are brought together under a shared head-line which underscores the conceptual links, and the public con-flation, between the idea of the child and the idea of society:

'TRAGIC PROOF THAT SOCIETY HAS LOST ITS SOUL.'

Writing in the same edition of the newspaper, Walter Schwarz concludes that if public consciousness has been stirred:

'it is because children in a moral vacuum seem the most spectacular victims of a society in which people have ceased officially to count.'

(Guardian, 27 November 1993)

The events of November 1993 thus yielded a three-fold restatement and confirmation of what, in the public mind, children are as the loss of childhood itself seemed immanent. First, 'the child' is not evil; second, 'the child' is not adult; and third, 'the child' is a symbol of society's optimism, a search for a hopeful future or a recollection of good times past. Because of this, children who commit acts of violence were by definition firmly excluded from the conceptual category of 'child'. Through their actions, such children contravene its boundaries and in so doing threaten, most fundamentally, each of our senses of attach-ment to the social bond.

WHAT DOES THE CHILD NEED?

The differing accounts as to why and how it is possible for children to commit crimes of violence were, as has been shown, partially synthesized in public perceptions through the redrawing of the traditional boundaries of childhood. While this momen-tarily dissolved the conundrum, it offered little comfort for the future. Thus it was in pursuit of a solution to, rather than simply an explanation of, the conceptual problem posed by children not behaving as children that the broad band of public opinion widened to ask more searching questions about childhood. Views about what children need ranged from a harshly repressive response to a more liberal one.

For those who would pinpoint evil nature as the locus of violence in some children, repression and retribution were simple solutions:

'We must recognise, and act to ensure that, society is protected from evil individuals of whatever age. If criminals act against society then they must be removed from society.'

(*Guardian*, 27 November 1993)

Predictably, similar calls have been made before. In 1989 after the assault of a paralysed woman by three boys, aged nine, seven and six, a superintendent of police remarked that:

'We would like to see the age of criminality lowered and we would like to see the boys facing criminal action.'

(*Guardian*, 13 April 1989)

For those others who would espouse a more liberal viewpoint, preferring to blame society as the legitimating source of some children's violence, the solution was less individualized and certainly less clear cut.

'Parents cannot cope and schools are left without adequate resources or training to pick up the pieces. Year after year the same patterns of behaviour recur. There is all too frequently nowhere for disturbed children to go, so they do not get the care and treatment they need. As a society we are failing all our children if we do not have the will and the commitment to enable them to grow up with the support and guidance they need.'

(*Guardian*, 27 November 1993)

Thus, between, on the one hand, the clamour for punishment, revenge and retribution and, on the other hand, demands for understanding and loving care, it would seem that public perceptions of what children need are indeed in disarray. And this is not a peculiarly British problem. In France, despite the collective assertion that children who commit violent crimes are still children and cannot be held responsible, a similar dilemma remains about what measures might be taken to prevent children committing acts of violence.

If, as Woodhead[36] has argued, concepts of children's needs are integral to the social construction of childhood itself, then the collective indecision and social paralysis previously discussed, becomes comprehensible. As a society, and presumably as individuals, we do not know what actions to take because we do not know what children are. They are steadily slipping from our conceptual grasp, and because we no longer know what children are then we can neither understand nor articulate their needs.

WHAT CAN BE DONE?

What can be done is complex and, as yet, uncertain. But what is being done, in the name of prevention, is both simple and deceptively straightforward. As ever with contemporary crisis management, we witness a convenient 'scapegoating', the searching out of something or somebody to blame. The targets have been as banal as the unspecified causality of video games and their suspicious 'hyperreality', lack of discipline in homes and schools, declining standards of morality, and truancy. All these are seen as key antagonistic elements in the battle to recover the lost innocence of children, explanatory devices dedicated to recreating yesterday's children not to forging tomorrow's adults.

Taking the lead from the Bulger trial judge's remarks in November 1993, the Government's response to the growing moral panic about the nation's children has been to establish a set of controls upon children's activities. 'Truancy Watch', launched in autumn 1993, is designed to encourage the public policing of children and takes its cue from a scheme already running 'successfully' in Stoke-on-Trent:

> 'Shops display "truant-free zone" stickers and staff are trained to challenge suspects and fill in confidential forms for education welfare officers. Buses carry posters asking: "Are you sure your child is in school?" '
>
> (*Guardian*, 27 November 1993)

The resonances with Foucault's panopticon are clear. Truancy Watch has been described by the teacher's unions as being akin to:

'unleashing "an army of spies and informants into the streets".'

(*Guardian*, 27 November 1993)

Such public accountability for children represents a revival of concepts of 'the child' as public property taking us back to the pragmatic origins of mass education, the economic policy of 'human capital' and the educational ideology of vocationalism. A diffuse and spurious sense of the collective is invoked in political discourse and charged with the role of 'guardian of the nation's future'. All these are paradoxical claims in the face of earlier Government pronouncements concerning the rolling back of the State and the celebration of individualism. This confused response was, however, put forward by John Patten, Secretary of State for Education, in the autumn of 1993:

'Until such time as we can rely on all parents to fulfil their side of the bargain there is going to be an important role for the community.'

(*Guardian*, 27 November 1993)

Such a brand of community care may have a continuity with the now disbanded policy of mobilizing a 'Mum's Army' for infant education, but it is very much at odds with the spirit of the newly instituted Children Act whose enlightened philosophy strains towards the child's liberty rather than its further containment. Similarly, the call for the restriction of children's access to video games and films as being the 'likely' source of illicit knowledge which prematurely ages children's minds, may run counter to more liberal or, indeed, more informed claims – for example, the call for children's increased need for earlier sex education, a demand being made currently in response to growing numbers of schoolgirl pregnancies and the threats to health posed by HIV and AIDS. A similar polarity centres around the value of school uniform as a deterrent to truancy and a method of social control as against the child's freedom to self-expression through the opening up of choice. But such stabs at reform or social engineering offer few solutions. They are mostly about containment. They universally fail to resolve a more central problematic: if we don't know what children are, then we don't know what they need and, if we don't know what they need then . . .? What?

There is, however, one way out of this dilemma which has still to be fully explored. Yet, unless the socially constructed nature of childhood becomes more widely registered, it is an opportunity which may not even be taken. One way of discovering why children commit acts of violence, what motivates them or what stays their hands, would be to know more from children themselves about crime and violence. Just as in the 1980s when child sexual abuse was high up the agenda we found that we did not know much about the extent of children's knowledge about sex, so also now the adult world finds itself in a state of ignorance about what ordinary children do ordinarily to one another. For example, an emerging body of work from the USA indicates that most child abuse, sexual, physical and psychological, is, in fact, peer abuse.[37] We need to know what bullying is and how and why it occurs; when does teasing become bullying and when does taunting turn to violence? But to ask children such questions is, unsurprisingly, a course of action fraught with conceptual problems and perhaps even ethical problems.

Given the dominance of particular models of child development in public perceptions of children, models which are both unilinear and on the whole uniform, children are rarely seen as competent advocates of their own experiences.[38] Children as social actors may gradually becoming visible and acceptable within sociology but in the public world children themselves may still have little opportunity to have their voices listened to. Children's words may continue to be viewed with suspicion, or indifference, by an adult audience as in cases of child sexual abuse where age, rather than experience, may still often be deemed the more important indicator of a child's ability to tell, or even know, the truth. Thus, in trying to ask children about violent crime, would what they have to say be judged as insightful or would it be tempered, even nullified, by adult listeners? And should what children have to say prove unacceptable to the adult world, with what value would it be credited? Would it be simply dismissed as evidence of children's inability to be articulate observers, further justification for not including them in decisions made about their welfare? These problems are real, but not insurmountable as ethnographic work with children by sociologists and anthropologists is beginning to demonstrate.

To my knowledge there has been just one public attempt to ask children about violent crime and the tone of its reporting hints at the unacceptability of the responses which were obtained. Under the headline 'Bulger: chill verdict of the children', Charles Hymas recounted what he terms as the 'cynical' opinions of the young people with whom he talked. He expressed surprise at their 'moralistic, even reactionary' attitudes:

> 'Everybody is responsible for their own thoughts and the way they deal with these thoughts. The kids were wrong and they got what they deserved. They have nobody else to blame apart from themselves.'
>
> (*The Sunday Times*, 5 December 1993)

That children should express the attitude that 'basically society is better off without them', that the punishment given to the child murderers 'was not severe enough', poses a conceptual problem for Hymas. But his problem is also ours. Is the punitive line taken by these children merely a callow replication of received views, a sign of their immaturity and lack of experience; is it, as it were, a sign of their innocent immaturity? Or, more troubling perhaps, might their desire for revenge and harsh justice be an indication of a cruel propensity in all children, the image entertained by adults only through fiction from *The Midwich Cuckoos* to *The Lord of the Flies*? If so, then our traditional idea of 'the child' must be abandoned. If not, then surely we have to reject any monolithic category of 'the child' and work instead with the more pluralistic concepts of 'childhoods', 'children' and 'childlikeness'? But to abandon a shared category of the child is to confront a daunting paradox. If as adults we do just that, what happens to the concept of 'childhood' through which we, as adults, see ourselves and our society's past and future? If, as we have argued here, the concept of 'childhood' serves to articulate not just the experience and status of the young within modern society but also the projections, aspirations, longings and altruism contained within the adult experience then to abandon such a conception is to erase our final point of stability and attachment to the social bond. In a historical era during which issues of identity and integration[39] are, perhaps, both more unstable and more fragile than at any previous time such a loss would impact upon the everyday experience of societal members with disorienting consequences. Only by interrogating the possessive adhesion of adults to the concept of childhood in the context of post-modernity, can we begin to understand the fear behind those distorted masks of hatred and retribution that disfigured the faces of the crowd outside of the South Sefton Magistrates' Court in Bootle during 1993 where two sad little boys were being charged with the murder of a third.

NOTES

[1] The body of the arguments and data put forward in this chapter previously appeared in a paper that I jointly authored with **Allison James** from the Department of Sociology and Social Anthropology at the University of Hull. We first presented it as 'Public perceptions of childhood criminality' at a Childhood and Society seminar, 15 April 1994, at the University of Keele. She has my gratitude for allowing me to include it in this volume of my own work and my appreciation for our continued collaboration.

[2] N. Postman, *The Disappearance of Childhood*, New York: Vintage Books, 1994, p. xi.

[3] V. Marchant, *A National Survey of Computer Pornography in Schools*, University of Central Lancashire, 1994.

[4] N. Postman, op. cit., p. 120.

[5] S. Kline, *Out of the Garden: Toys, TV and Children's Culture in the Age of Marketing*, London: Verso, 1993; D. Buckingham, 'Television and the definition of childhood' in B. Mayall (ed.), *Children's Childhoods: Observed and Experienced*, London: Falmer, 1994.

[6] M. Thomas, *Every Mother's Nightmare*, London: Pan, 1993, p. 1.

[7] Mary Bell served eleven years and five months of her 'life' sentence before release and is now married with two children of her own.

[8] D. Harrison, 'Unbelievably evil', in the *Observer*, 18 June 1995, p. 19.

[9] A. James, 'On being a child: the self, the group and the category' in A. P. Cohen and N. J. Rapport (eds), *Questions of Consciousness*, London: Routledge, 1994.

[10] P. Ariès, *Centuries of Childhood*, Harmondsworth: Penguin, 1962.

[11] See also L. DeMause (ed.), *The History of Childhood*, London: Souvenir Press, 1976; L. Stone, *The Family, Sex and Marriage in England 1500–1800*, London: Weidenfeld & Nicolson, 1977; L. Pollock, *Forgotten Children: Parent–Child Relations from 1500 to 1900*, Cambridge: Cambridge University Press, 1983; J. Demos, *Past, Present and Personal*, Oxford: Oxford University Press, 1986; R. Houlbrooke, *The English Family 1450–1700*, London: Longman, 1984; J. Boswell, *The Kindness of Strangers: the Abandonment of*

Children in Western Europe from Late Antiquity to the Renaissance, Harmondsworth: Penguin, 1988.

[12] R. Sennet, *The Fall of Public Man*, London: Faber & Faber, 1993, p. 92.

[13] A. James and A. Prout (eds), *Constructing and Reconstructing Childhood*, Basingstoke: Falmer, 1990; A. James, *Childhood Identities: Self and Social Relations in the Experience of the Child*, Edinburgh: Edinburgh University Press, 1993.

[14] C. Jenks (ed.), *The Sociology of Childhood*, London: Batsford, 1982.

[15] J. Ennew, *The Sexual Exploitation of Children*, Cambridge: Polity Press, 1986, p. 21.

[16] D. Armstrong, *Political Anatomy of the Body: Medical Knowledge in Britain in the Twentieth Century*, Cambridge: Cambridge University Press, 1983.

[17] J. Boyden, 'Childhood and the policy makers: a comparative perspective on the globalization of childhood' in A. James and A. Prout (eds), op. cit.

[18] J. Ennew, op. cit., p. 21.

[19] M. Last, 'Putting children first' in *Disasters*, vol. 18, no. 3, 1994.

[20] J. Hockey and A. James, *Growing Up and Growing Old: Ageing and Dependency in the Life Course*, London: Sage, 1993.

[21] S. Freud, *Three Essays on the Theory of Sexuality* (1905) (trans. J. Strachey), London: Imago Press, 1949.

[22] H. Hendrick, 'Constructions and reconstructions of British childhood: an interpretive study 1800 to the present' in A. James and A. Prout (eds), op. cit.

[23] J. Kitzinger, 'Who are you kidding? Children, power and the struggle against sexual abuse' in A. James and A. Prout (eds), op. cit.

[24] E. Burman, 'Innocents abroad: Western fantasies of children and the iconography of emergencies' in *Disasters*, vol. 18, no. 3, 1994.

[25] S. Johnson, *The Independent*, 22 December 1994, p. 18.

[26] C. Jenks, 'Child abuse in the postmodern context: an issue of social identity' in *Childhood*, no. 2, 1994, pp. 111–121.

[27] N. Rose, *Governing the Soul*, London: Routledge, 1989; J. Donzelot, *The Policing of Families*, London: Hutchinson, 1986.

[28] M. Foucault, *Discipline and Punish*, London: Allen Lane, 1973.

[29] P. Virilio, *Speed and Politics*, New York: Semiotext(e), 1986.

[30] U. Beck, *Risk Society: Towards a New Modernity*, London: Sage, 1992.

[31] M. Douglas, *Risk and Blame: Essays in Cultural Theory*, London: Routledge, 1994, p. 46.

[32] M. Douglas, *Purity and Danger*, Harmondsworth: Penguin, 1970.

[33] Ibid., p. 136.

[34] Ibid., p. 137.

[35] A. Giddens, *Modernity and Self-Identity*, Cambridge: Polity Press, 1991.

[36] M. Woodhead, 'Psychology and the cultural construction of children's needs' in A. James and A. Prout (eds), op. cit.

[37] A.-M. Ambert, 'The problem of peer abuse' in *Sociological Studies of Children*, vol. 7, Greenwich, CT: JAI Press, 1995.

[38] C. Jenks, 'Decoding childhood' in P. Atkinson, S. Delamont and B. Davies (eds), *Discourse and Reproduction: Essays in Honour of Basil Bernstein*, New York: Hampton Press, 1995.

[39] A. Giddens, op. cit.

Postscript

Margaret, are you grieving
Over Goldengrove unleaving?
Leaves, like the things of man, you
With your fresh thoughts care for, can you?
Ah! as the heart grows older
It will come to such sights colder
By and by, nor spare a sigh
Though worlds of wanwood leafmeal lie;
And yet you will weep and know why.
Now no matter, child, the name:
Sorrow's springs are the same.
Nor mouth had, no nor mind expressed
What heart heard of, ghost guessed:
It is the blight man was born for,
It is Margaret you mourn for.

Gerard Manley Hopkins *Spring and Fall: To a young child*

Index